CAMBRIDGE

Shakespeare

Measure
FOR
Measure

Edited by Jane Coles and Rex Gibson

Series Editor: Rex Gibson
Director, Shakespeare and Schools Project

CAMBRIDGE
UNIVERSITY PRESS

Published by the Press Syndicate of the University of Cambridge
The Pitt Building, Trumpington Street, Cambridge CB2 1RP
40 West 20th Street, New York, NY 10011–4211, USA
10 Stamford Road, Oakleigh, Victoria 3166, Australia

First published 1993
Printed in Great Britain at the University Press, Cambridge

A catalogue record for this book is available from the British Library.

Library of Congress cataloguing in publication data applied for.

ISBN 0 521 42506 9 paperback

Prepared for publication by Stenton Associates
Designed by Richard Morris, Stonesfield Design
Picture research by Callie Kendall
Illustration by Jones and Sewell Associates

Thanks are due to the following for permission to reproduce photographs:

Jacket: Reg Wilson; 10, 100, 124, 170, 186, Shakespeare Centre Library, Stratford-upon-Avon: Joe Cocks Studio Collection; 14, 82, 104, Angus McBean; 36, 62*l*, 144, Shakespeare Centre Library, Stratford-upon-Avon; 44, 92, 103*r*, 110, Clive Barda/Performing Arts Library; 62*r*, Morris Newcombe; 66, Mansell Collection; 103*c*, Amanda Abegg; 103*l*, Reg Wilson; 112, The Master and Fellows, Magdalene College, Cambridge, Pepys Ballad Collection, Volume 2, page 153; 139, 181, By permission of the Syndics of the Cambridge University Library/British Library; 179*t*, Courtesy of Royal Shakespeare Theatre.

Contents

Cambridge School Shakespeare

This edition of *Measure for Measure* is part of the *Cambridge School Shakespeare* series. Like every other play in the series, it has been specially prepared to help all students in schools and colleges.

This *Measure for Measure* aims to be different from other editions of the play. It invites you to bring the play to life in your classroom, hall or drama studio through enjoyable activities that will increase your understanding. Actors have created their different interpretations of the play over the centuries. Similarly, you are encouraged to make up your own mind about *Measure for Measure*, rather than having someone else's interpretation handed down to you.

Cambridge School Shakespeare does not offer you a cut-down or simplified version of the play. This is Shakespeare's language, filled with imaginative possibilities. You will find on every left-hand page: a summary of the action, an explanation of unfamiliar words, a choice of activities on Shakespeare's language, characters and stories.

Between each act and in the pages at the end of the play, you will find notes, illustrations and activities. These will help to increase your understanding of the whole play.

There are a large number of activities to give you the widest choice to suit your own particular needs. Please don't think you have to do every one. Choose the activities that will help you most.

This edition will be of value to you whether you are studying for an examination, reading for pleasure, or thinking of putting on the play to entertain others. You can work on the activities on your own or in groups. Many of the activities suggest a particular group size, but don't be afraid to make up larger or smaller groups to suit your own purposes.

Although you are invited to treat *Measure for Measure* as a play, you don't need special dramatic or theatrical skills to do the activities. By choosing your activities, and by exploring and experimenting, you can make your own interpretations of Shakespeare's language, characters and stories. Whatever you do, remember that Shakespeare wrote his plays to be acted, watched and enjoyed.

Rex Gibson

This edition of *Measure for Measure* uses the text of the play established by Brian Gibbons in *The New Cambridge Shakespeare*.

List of characters

VINCENTIO   Duke of Vienna

The Law

ANGELO   the Duke's Deputy
ESCALUS   an ancient Lord
PROVOST   warder of the prison
ELBOW   a simple constable
ABHORSON   an executioner
JUSTICE   assistant to Escalus

The Citizens

ISABELLA   a novice nun
CLAUDIO   her brother
JULIET   beloved of Claudio
LUCIO   friend of Claudio
TWO GENTLEMEN
MARIANA   formerly betrothed to Angelo

The Brothel and the Prison

FROTH   a foolish gentleman
POMPEY   a pimp and tapster
MISTRESS OVERDONE   a bawd (brothel-keeper)
BARNARDINE   an imprisoned murderer

The Church

FRIAR THOMAS ⎱
FRIAR PETER   ⎰ Franciscan friars
FRANCISCA   a Sister of the Poor Clares

Other characters: Varrius (friend of the Duke), Lords, Officers, Servants, Citizens, a Boy

The action of the play takes place in Vienna and at the moated grange (a secluded country house).

Duke Vincentio praises Escalus's political wisdom and knowledge of Vienna's people, customs and laws. The Duke reveals that he has appointed Angelo to rule the city in his absence.

1 First sight of the Duke (in pairs)

The Royal Shakespeare Company's 1987 production opened with a long silence. The Duke, pen in hand, sat trembling and sweating, obviously nervous. In the distance a prison door was heard clanging shut. At last, just before he spoke, the Duke, still trembling, signed an official document on his desk.

- Read aloud the Duke's lines 3–21. Try saying them in a confident manner, then in a nervous, hesitant manner. Try other styles (for example, pompously or humorously). Which tone do you think is most appropriate?
- Read the lines aloud again. Emphasise every time the Duke refers to himself in the first person ('I', 'me', and so on) or in the plural, the language of royalty ('our', 'we', 'us'). Talk together about what you discover about how he uses personal ('I') and formal ('we') language.
- What is your first impression of the Duke? How would you stage it?

2 What's the play going to be about? (in small groups)

Many people believe that the opening scene of each Shakespeare play announces central themes of the play. Here clues could be: 'government' (line 3); 'justice' (line 11); the absent ruler (line 18); the substitute ruler (lines 18–21). Use each of these clues to predict to each other how you think the play will develop.

3 A printer's error?

If you found line 8 difficult to understand, don't worry – so does everyone else. Perhaps the first printer (in 1623) made an error. Or perhaps the obscurity gives a clue to the character of the Duke. One meaning is 'but add my authority to your skill'.

---

properties essential qualities
t'affect to show off with
am put to know acknowledge
science knowledge
sufficiency authority
able given power

pregnant in knowledgeable about
commission document that
 delegates power
warp deviate
terror dread power
deputation position as deputy

Measure for Measure

ACT 1   SCENE 1
Vienna   The Duke's Palace

Enter DUKE, ESCALUS, LORDS

DUKE Escalus.
ESCALUS My lord.
DUKE Of government the properties to unfold
    Would seem in me t'affect speech and discourse,
    Since I am put to know that your own science   5
    Exceeds, in that, the lists of all advice
    My strength can give you. Then no more remains
    But that, to your sufficiency, as your worth is able,
    And let them work. The nature of our people,
    Our city's institutions, and the terms   10
    For common justice, y'are as pregnant in
    As art and practice hath enrichèd any
    That we remember. There is our commission,
    From which we would not have you warp. Call hither,
    I say, bid come before us Angelo.   15

                                           [*Exit a Lord*]

    What figure of us think you he will bear?
    For you must know, we have with special soul
    Elected him our absence to supply,
    Lent him our terror, dressed him with our love,
    And given his deputation all the organs   20
    Of our own power. What think you of it?
ESCALUS If any in Vienna be of worth
    To undergo such ample grace and honour
    It is Lord Angelo.

Enter ANGELO

DUKE   Look where he comes.
ANGELO Always obedient to your grace's will   25
    I come to know your pleasure.

The Duke says Angelo's qualities are obvious for all to see. He argues that natural talents should be used, not hoarded. Appointing Angelo as substitute ruler, the Duke prepares to leave at once.

1 Don't hide your light under a bushel! (in pairs)

The Duke advises Angelo to use and develop his talents, not to keep them to himself (lines 29–40). His words echo parables from the Bible (Matthew 5 and 25: the parables of the candlestick and the talents). Read the lines to each other several times in different ways:

as a preacher to a congregation   as a boss to an employee
as a parent to a son or daughter   as a teacher lecturing to a class.

After your readings, talk together about how you think the Duke would have spoken the lines to Angelo.

2 Money, money, money

Images of money, coins and forgery echo through the play. On the opposite page the Duke or Angelo speak of 'finely touched', 'fine issues', 'lends', 'thrifty', 'creditor', 'test', 'metal', 'noble', 'figure', 'stamped'.

Gold coins (known as 'Angels' or angel-nobles) were issued after being assayed (tested with a touchstone) as fine (genuine). An image (figure) was stamped on them of St Michael, the archangel, killing the dragon. They were given to sick people who were 'touched' for the King's Evil. Angelo's 'metal' is a pun on mettle (spirit).

Look out for other references to coins in the play. Will Angelo prove to be true gold or a forgery?

---

character obvious sign
thyself . . . thee your qualities are not simply your own to use selfishly
go forth of us show in practice
spirits . . . issues only great moral causes inspire noble emotions

nature . . . use Nature bestows talents, but insists they are used and increased
scruple tiny weight
advertise instruct
leavened mature

4

DUKE   Angelo:
There is a kind of character in thy life
That to th'observer doth thy history
Fully unfold. Thyself and thy belongings
Are not thine own so proper as to waste   30
Thyself upon thy virtues, they on thee.
Heaven doth with us as we with torches do,
Not light them for themselves: for if our virtues
Did not go forth of us, 'twere all alike
As if we had them not. Spirits are not finely touched   35
But to fine issues: nor nature never lends
The smallest scruple of her excellence
But, like a thrifty goddess, she determines
Herself the glory of a creditor,
Both thanks and use. But I do bend my speech   40
To one that can my part in him advertise.
Hold therefore, Angelo:
In our remove be thou at full ourself.
Mortality and mercy in Vienna
Live in thy tongue and heart. Old Escalus,   45
Though first in question, is thy secondary.
Take thy commission.
ANGELO   Now good my lord,
Let there be some more test made of my metal
Before so noble and so great a figure
Be stamped upon it.
DUKE   No more evasion.   50
We have with a leavened and preparèd choice
Proceeded to you; therefore take your honours.
Our haste from hence is of so quick condition
That it prefers itself and leaves unquestioned
Matters of needful value. We shall write to you,   55
As time and our concernings shall importune,
How it goes with us, and do look to know
What doth befall you here. So fare you well.
To th'hopeful execution do I leave you
Of your commissions.

The Duke wishes to leave alone, at once. He says he dislikes public appearances and prefers a secret departure. Angelo and Escalus resolve to discover the precise nature of their powers.

---

1 Handing over power/taking over power

Angelo has just been given supreme power in Vienna. What will he do? Imagine that the Head or Principal of your school or college has just handed over her/his authority to you. Decide the very first act you'll do with your new power.

Now imagine that you've suddenly been appointed supreme political leader of your country. What will be your first act – and why? Compare your decisions with others'.

2 Why is the Duke leaving? (in groups of four)

At this moment in the play, it's not clear why the Duke is leaving in such a hurry. Talk together about possible reasons for his hasty departure and handing over of power. Also discuss why neither Angelo nor Escalus asks where he's going. As you read on, check if your guesses are justified.

3 Was Shakespeare flattering King James?

King James I was the patron of Shakespeare's acting company ('The King's Men'). The first performance of *Measure for Measure* may have been in 1604 in the Banqueting Hall of the Palace of Westminster, with King James in the audience. Lines 67–72 may refer to him (his dislike of crowds was well known).

- How likely do you think it is that Shakespeare was flattering King James in the play?
- Research the character of King James (you'll find help on page 176). Speculate whether he would be susceptible to flattery by a playwright.

---

something on part of
Nor need . . . scruple Don't feel doubt
scope power, freedom to act
privily privately
aves welcoming shouts (ave = Hail, Latin)

of safe discretion trustworthy
affect enjoy
look . . . place find out fully my duties and authority

ANGELO   Yet give leave, my lord,   60
    That we may bring you something on the way.
DUKE My haste may not admit it,
    Nor need you, on mine honour, have to do
    With any scruple. Your scope is as mine own
    So to enforce or qualify the laws   65
    As to your soul seems good. Give me your hand,
    I'll privily away. I love the people,
    But do not like to stage me to their eyes:
    Though it do well I do not relish well
    Their loud applause and aves vehement,   70
    Nor do I think the man of safe discretion
    That does affect it. Once more, fare you well.
ANGELO The heavens give safety to your purposes.
ESCALUS Lead forth and bring you back in happiness.
DUKE I thank you, fare you well.   *Exit* 75
ESCALUS I shall desire you, sir, to give me leave
    To have free speech with you; and it concerns me
    To look into the bottom of my place.
    A power I have, but of what strength and nature
    I am not yet instructed.   80
ANGELO 'Tis so with me. Let us withdraw together
    And we may soon our satisfaction have
    Touching that point.
ESCALUS   I'll wait upon your honour.
                                             Exeunt

Lucio and two Gentlemen joke together, trying to score points off each other. The first Gentleman implies that Lucio has a sexually transmitted disease.

1 Cross-talk comedy? (in groups of three)

Fashions in humour change quickly. Jokes are often concerned with topical events. To Shakespeare's audiences, much of the humour came from echoes of current affairs or puns about sex.

Read through the quickfire exchanges of lines 1–45 several times, changing roles. Then work on one or more of the following activities.

- Echoes of history: 'the King of Hungary' may be a veiled reference to the peace negotiations with Spain in 1604 (when Shakespeare probably wrote the play). Invent a present-day political reference for Lucio's first three lines that could make a modern audience laugh.

- Echoes of religion: One person reads aloud all lines 1–23. The others echo every word with a religious meaning. Try this several times, changing readers and echoes. How many biblical or religious references can you find?

- Echoes of sex: There are several jokes in lines 26–45 about sexual disease ('piled' = losing hair or haemorrhoids [piles]. Both were thought to be caused by syphilis [a sexually transmitted disease]. 'French velvet' = expensive French cloth or prostitute, or syphilis). Talk together about whether you think the joking is similar to the way young men talk today.

- Echoes of measure: On every page of the play you will find an echo of the play's title: one thing or person being weighed against another. Here, the First Gentleman's 'there went but a pair of shears between us' ('we are the same') weighs Lucio and himself equally. Look out for this constant 'weighing' as you read the play.

---

composition agreement
fall upon will attack
table list (of the Ten Commandments)
razed erased
proportion rhythm
Grace God's merciful love

lists worthless pieces of cloth (edges cut off and thrown away)
velvet expensive cloth
three-piled expensive cloth
as lief rather
kersey coarse woollen cloth

ACT 1   SCENE 2
Vienna   A street

Enter LUCIO, and two other GENTLEMEN

LUCIO If the Duke, with the other dukes, come not to composition
with the King of Hungary, why then all the dukes fall upon the
King.

1 GENTLEMAN Heaven grant us its peace, but not the King of
Hungary's.   5

2 GENTLEMAN Amen.

LUCIO Thou conclud'st like the sanctimonious pirate that went to sea
with the ten commandments, but scraped one out of the table.

2 GENTLEMAN Thou shalt not steal?

LUCIO Ay, that he razed.   10

1 GENTLEMAN Why, 'twas a commandment to command the captain
and all the rest from their functions: they put forth to steal.
There's not a soldier of us all that, in the thanksgiving before
meat, do relish the petition well that prays for peace.

2 GENTLEMAN I never heard any soldier dislike it.   15

LUCIO I believe thee, for I think thou never wast where grace was said.

2 GENTLEMAN No? A dozen times at least.

1 GENTLEMAN What? In metre?

LUCIO In any proportion, or in any language.

1 GENTLEMAN I think, or in any religion.   20

LUCIO Ay? Why not? Grace is grace, despite of all controversy: as,
for example, thou thyself art a wicked villain, despite of all grace.

1 GENTLEMAN Well, there went but a pair of shears between us.

LUCIO I grant: as there may between the lists and the velvet. Thou
art the list.   25

1 GENTLEMAN And thou the velvet. Thou art good velvet: thou'rt a
three-piled piece, I warrant thee. I had as lief be a list of an
English kersey as be piled, as thou art piled, for a French velvet.
Do I speak feelingly now?

Lucio and the Gentlemen continue to accuse each other of having sexual diseases. Mistress Overdone tells them that Claudio is imprisoned and condemned to death for making Juliet pregnant.

What's in a name? Lucio calls Mistress Overdone 'Madam Mitigation'. Her services as a brothel-keeper (Bawd) satisfy or mitigate sexual lust. How else does her name signify her profession? The photograph shows how she was portrayed in the 1962 Royal Shakespeare Company's production. Is this how you imagine her? Talk together about how you think she should enter and behave before she speaks her first words at line 49.

---

begin drink to
forget to . . . thee I wouldn't drink
  out of your glass
dolours diseases (a pun on dollars)
French crown bald head (believed
  to be caused by syphilis)

figuring imagining
impiety wickedness
the proclamation public statement
  of law-enforcement

LUCIO I think thou dost, and indeed with most painful feeling of thy   30
speech. I will, out of thine own confession, learn to begin thy
health; but, whilst I live, forget to drink after thee.

1 GENTLEMAN I think I have done myself wrong, have I not?

2 GENTLEMAN Yes, that thou hast, whether thou art tainted or free.

Enter [MISTRESS OVERDONE, *a*] *Bawd*

LUCIO Behold, behold, where Madam Mitigation comes. I have   35
purchased as many diseases under her roof as come to –

2 GENTLEMAN To what, I pray?

LUCIO Judge.

2 GENTLEMAN To three thousand dolours a year.

1 GENTLEMAN Ay, and more.   40

LUCIO A French crown more.

1 GENTLEMAN Thou art always figuring diseases in me, but thou art
full of error: I am sound.

LUCIO Nay, not, as one would say, healthy, but so sound as things
that are hollow. Thy bones are hollow. Impiety has made a feast   45
of thee.

1 GENTLEMAN How now, which of your hips has the most profound
sciatica?

MISTRESS OVERDONE Well, well: there's one yonder arrested and
carried to prison was worth five thousand of you all.   50

2 GENTLEMAN Who's that, I pray thee?

MISTRESS OVERDONE Marry, sir, that's Claudio, Signior Claudio.

1 GENTLEMAN Claudio to prison? 'Tis not so.

MISTRESS OVERDONE Nay, but I know 'tis so. I saw him arrested,
saw him carried away, and, which is more, within these three   55
days his head to be chopped off!

LUCIO But, after all this fooling, I would not have it so. Art thou sure
of this?

MISTRESS OVERDONE I am too sure of it: and it is for getting
Madam Julietta with child.   60

LUCIO Believe me, this may be. He promised to meet me two hours
since, and he was ever precise in promise-keeping.

2 GENTLEMAN Besides, you know, it draws something near to the
speech we had to such a purpose.

1 GENTLEMAN But most of all agreeing with the proclamation.   65

LUCIO Away. Let's go learn the truth of it.

Exeunt Lucio [*and Gentlemen*]

Mistress Overdone complains that she is short of customers. Pompey tells her of Claudio's offence and that the brothels are to be demolished. Claudio is led in, protesting at being on public display.

1 Mistress Overdone's complaint (in groups of four to six)

Create five tableaux (frozen pictures), to show the five things of which Mistress Overdone complains in lines 67–9.

Each group shows its five tableaux to the rest of the class. Discuss what they suggest to you about Shakespeare's Vienna – and the London of his time (see illustration on page 29).

2 How do they speak? (in pairs)

Take parts and read Pompey's and Mistress Overdone's conversation. Change roles and repeat. Agree together on how you think they speak.

3 Did Shakespeare forget?

In line 74, Mistress Overdone asks what is Claudio's offence, but she already knows (lines 59–60). If you were directing the play, what advice would you give to the actor playing Mistress Overdone when she asks you about this puzzle?

4 'Worn your eyes almost out' (line 92)

Pompey's joke uses the image of Blind Cupid. Each London brothel in Shakespeare's day had its own sign (like a modern inn sign). Blind or blindfolded Cupid, god of love, was a popular symbol.

Do you think Pompey is taunting Mistress Overdone or genuinely comforting her? Or does he have other intentions in mind?

---

the sweat a treatment for syphilis (sweating in tubs)
Groping . . . river sexual intercourse
houses brothels
seed seed corn (to ensure the continuance of prostitution)

a wise burgher . . . them a speculator bought them
good counsellors brothels and prostitutes
tapster barman
the service prostitution

MISTRESS OVERDONE Thus, what with the war, what with the sweat, what with the gallows, and what with poverty, I am custom-shrunk.

Enter [POMPEY]

How now? What's the news with you?   70
POMPEY Yonder man is carried to prison.
MISTRESS OVERDONE Well, what has he done?
POMPEY A woman.
MISTRESS OVERDONE But what's his offence?
POMPEY Groping for trouts in a peculiar river.   75
MISTRESS OVERDONE What? Is there a maid with child by him?
POMPEY No, but there's a woman with maid by him. You have not heard of the proclamation, have you?
MISTRESS OVERDONE What proclamation, man?
POMPEY All houses in the suburbs of Vienna must be plucked down. 80
MISTRESS OVERDONE And what shall become of those in the city?
POMPEY They shall stand for seed. They had gone down too, but that a wise burgher put in for them.
MISTRESS OVERDONE But shall all our houses of resort in the suburbs be pulled down?   85
POMPEY To the ground, mistress.
MISTRESS OVERDONE Why, here's a change indeed in the commonwealth. What shall become of me?
POMPEY Come, fear not you: good counsellors lack no clients. Though you change your place, you need not change your trade. 90
I'll be your tapster still. Courage, there will be pity taken on you, you that have worn your eyes almost out in the service, you will be considered.
MISTRESS OVERDONE What's to do here, Thomas Tapster? Let's withdraw.   95
POMPEY Here comes Signior Claudio, led by the provost to prison; and there's Madam Juliet.

Exeunt

Enter PROVOST, CLAUDIO, JULIET, OFFICERS, LUCIO, *and two* GENTLEMEN

CLAUDIO Fellow, why dost thou show me thus to th'world?
Bear me to prison, where I am committed.

Claudio tells Lucio that offenders will be punished, and that imprisonment results from too much freedom. His offence is getting Juliet pregnant before marriage.

1 Measure for measure

Imagine that your hands are a pair of scales. Read lines 102–12 aloud, 'weighing' or balancing the comparisons and contrasts Claudio makes.

2 Money or love?

In Shakespeare's day couples could be regarded as married ('a true contract') even if they had not had a church ceremony. Claudio and Juliet delayed their church marriage in order to obtain a dowry (gift of money) from their friends. Do you think that waiting for a money arrangement reflects on the quality of their love?

Claudio and Juliet under arrest (Shakespeare Memorial Theatre, 1950). Which characters can you identify?

evil disposition malice
surfeit excessive eating
scope freedom, licence
ravin down ravenously swallow
bane poison
as lief rather
looked after regarded, punished

fast securely
denunciation public announcement
propagation increase
dower dowry (marriage settlement)
coffer box for money

PROVOST I do it not in evil disposition, 100
        But from Lord Angelo by special charge.
CLAUDIO Thus can the demi-god, Authority,
        Make us pay down for our offence by weight
        The words of heaven; on whom it will, it will,
        On whom it will not, so; yet still 'tis just. 105
LUCIO Why, how now, Claudio? Whence comes this restraint?
CLAUDIO From too much liberty, my Lucio, liberty.
        As surfeit is the father of much fast,
        So every scope by the immoderate use
        Turns to restraint. Our natures do pursue 110
        Like rats that ravin down their proper bane
        A thirsty evil, and when we drink, we die.
LUCIO If I could speak so wisely under an arrest, I would send for
    certain of my creditors; and yet, to say the truth, I had as lief have
    the foppery of freedom as the morality of imprisonment. What's 115
    thy offence, Claudio?
CLAUDIO What but to speak of would offend again.
LUCIO What, is't murder?
CLAUDIO No.
LUCIO Lechery? 120
CLAUDIO Call it so.
PROVOST Away, sir, you must go.
CLAUDIO One word, good friend: Lucio, a word with you.
LUCIO A hundred, if they'll do you any good. Is lechery so looked
    after? 125
CLAUDIO Thus stands it with me. Upon a true contract
        I got possession of Julietta's bed –
        You know the lady, she is fast my wife,
        Save that we do the denunciation lack
        Of outward order. This we came not to 130
        Only for propagation of a dower
        Remaining in the coffer of her friends,
        From whom we thought it meet to hide our love
        Till time had made them for us. But it chances
        The stealth of our most mutual entertainment 135
        With character too gross is writ on Juliet.

Claudio speculates on Angelo's reasons for reviving long-neglected laws against sex before marriage. He decides Angelo wishes to enhance his reputation. He asks Lucio to persuade Isabella to plead for his life.

1 The silent Juliet (in pairs)

Imagine that you are directing the play. The actor playing Juliet says to you, 'Look, I don't have a word to say in this scene, but I'm on stage for the last half of it. What do I do?'

Advise her on how she could behave at five or six points between lines 98 and 174.

2 Angelo's motivation (in small groups)

Claudio suggests four possible reasons (lines 139–45) why Angelo has revived the old law. Identify them, then talk together about whether you agree with Claudio's conclusion in line 152.

3 What is Claudio like? (in pairs)

Try different ways of speaking all Claudio says from line 98: bitter, angry, relaxed, resigned, amused by his predicament. Explore other moods. Does his tone change from speech to speech? Experiment!

4 First news of Isabella

Claudio gives three major pieces of information about Isabella in lines 158–67. Use them to write a few sentences on what you think Isabella will be like.

5 Two Gentlemen of Vienna (in pairs)

The two Gentlemen now disappear from the play. Improvise their conversation as they remind each other of all they can remember.

---

the fault and glimpse of newness the blame lies in Angelo's being dazzled by his new honour
body public state
place office, position
eminence personal ambition
I stagger in I'm not sure
zodiacs years

for a name to make a reputation
receive her approbation begin her probation as a novice nun
assay reason with
tick-tack a game in which scoring is by a peg placed in a hole (and so, a sexual innuendo)

LUCIO With child, perhaps?
CLAUDIO   Unhappily, even so.
        And the new deputy now for the Duke –
        Whether it be the fault and glimpse of newness,
        Or whether that the body public be   140
        A horse whereon the governor doth ride,
        Who, newly in the seat, that it may know
        He can command, lets it straight feel the spur;
        Whether the tyranny be in his place,
        Or in his eminence that fills it up,   145
        I stagger in – but this new governor
        Awakes me all the enrollèd penalties
        Which have, like unscoured armour, hung by th'wall
        So long that nineteen zodiacs have gone round
        And none of them been worn; and for a name   150
        Now puts the drowsy and neglected Act
        Freshly on me: 'tis surely for a name.
LUCIO I warrant it is; and thy head stands so tickle on thy shoulders
    that a milkmaid, if she be in love, may sigh it off. Send after the
    Duke and appeal to him.   155
CLAUDIO I have done so, but he's not to be found.
        I prithee, Lucio, do me this kind service:
        This day my sister should the cloister enter
        And there receive her approbation.
        Acquaint her with the danger of my state,   160
        Implore her, in my voice, that she make friends
        To the strict deputy: bid herself assay him.
        I have great hope in that; for in her youth
        There is a prone and speechless dialect
        Such as move men; beside, she hath prosperous art   165
        When she will play with reason and discourse,
        And well she can persuade.
LUCIO I pray she may, as well for the encouragement of the like,
    which else would stand under grievous imposition, as for the
    enjoying of thy life, who I would be sorry should be thus foolishly   170
    lost at a game of tick-tack. I'll to her.
CLAUDIO I thank you, good friend Lucio.
LUCIO Within two hours.
CLAUDIO Come, officer, away.
                                                                  Exeunt

17

The Duke denies that he is in love. He speaks of his dislike of crowds, of his delegation of power to Angelo, and of how his neglect of Vienna's strict laws has led to disorder and anarchy.

This short scene reveals the Duke's reasons for handing over power to Angelo. To gain a first impression, read the whole scene twice, taking turns to be the Duke. Then choose one of the following activities:

1 Friar Thomas's guess (in pairs)

Shakespeare occasionally began scenes in the middle of a conversation. Here, Friar Thomas has obviously just made a guess at why the Duke requires 'secret harbour'.

What was Friar Thomas's suggestion that made the Duke so flatly answer 'No'? Improvise the preceding conversation or write four lines in verse for Friar Thomas's suggestion.

2 Corrupt Vienna (in groups of six to eight)

In lines 20–32 the Duke gives a series of images, telling what has happened in Vienna. One person becomes the narrator, the others prepare a mime to act out each item in the Duke's description. You'll find you can show between eight and twelve actions.

3 Public duties and private preferences (in groups of four)

The Duke describes himself in lines 9–11. He prefers solitude, dislikes crowds where extravagantly dressed young people ('youth and cost') display in clothes or manners ('witless bravery'). But doesn't a ruler have to mix and take part in expensive ceremonial occasions? One person role-plays the Duke; the others cross-question him about the imbalance between his personal preferences and his public duties.

---

the dribbling dart of love Cupid's arrow
complete bosom perfect heart
the life removed the solitary life
strewed it rumoured
bits and curbs restraints

bound up . . . birch put away the rod
dead to infliction completely unenforced
liberty licence, anarchy
athwart awry, disordered

ACT 1 SCENE 3
Vienna A monastery

Enter DUKE *and* FRIAR THOMAS

DUKE No. Holy father, throw away that thought,
     Believe not that the dribbling dart of love
     Can pierce a complete bosom. Why I desire thee
     To give me secret harbour hath a purpose
     More grave and wrinkled than the aims and ends   5
     Of burning youth.
FRIAR May your grace speak of it?
DUKE My holy sir, none better knows than you
     How I have ever loved the life removed
     And held in idle price to haunt assemblies   10
     Where youth and cost witless bravery keeps.
     I have delivered to Lord Angelo,
     A man of stricture and firm abstinence,
     My absolute power and place here in Vienna,
     And he supposes me travelled to Poland –   15
     For so I have strewed it in the common ear,
     And so it is received. Now, pious sir,
     You will demand of me why I do this.
FRIAR Gladly, my lord.
DUKE We have strict statutes and most biting laws,   20
     The needful bits and curbs to headstrong weeds,
     Which for this fourteen years we have let slip,
     Even like an o'er-grown lion in a cave
     That goes not out to prey. Now, as fond fathers
     Having bound up the threatening twigs of birch   25
     Only to stick it in their children's sight
     For terror, not to use – in time the rod
     More mocked than feared – so our decrees,
     Dead to infliction, to themselves are dead,
     And Liberty plucks Justice by the nose,   30
     The baby beats the nurse, and quite athwart
     Goes all decorum.

The Duke explains that it would be tyrannical for him to punish the people now, because he has for so long neglected to enforce the law. He proposes to disguise himself as a friar to watch Angelo's rule.

1 Friar Thomas asks some questions (in pairs)

One partner is Friar Thomas, the other is the Duke. Friar Thomas questions the Duke on each part of his story, asking for clarification or justification. To help you, match this summary with lines 35–55:

- I neglected the laws
- So I shouldn't punish the people now
- Angelo can punish them in my name
- So I won't be slandered (or: I won't be around to slander him)
- I'll spy on Angelo and the people
- I'll disguise myself as a friar to do it
- I want to see if Angelo is really what he seems (or: I already suspect him).

Change roles and repeat. Are the same answers given?

2 'What our seemers be' (line 55) (in small groups)

'Seems' and 'seeming' will echo through the play. Is Angelo really like his outward appearance, or will power reveal what he truly is? Shakespeare explored the theme of the connection between appearance and reality in many of his plays. In *Macbeth*, Duncan says, 'There's no art to find the mind's construction in the face.' Hamlet says, 'Seems, madam! nay it is; I know not seems.'

In *Measure for Measure*, there's an immediate irony: the Duke, proposing to investigate Angelo's 'seeming', will disguise himself and seem to be what he is not!

Identify six things the Duke says about Angelo in this scene. Write a sentence or two about each characteristic, stating whether you think it is genuine or not.

---

scope liberty
strike and gall punish severely
have their permissive pass are allowed to occur
in th'ambush of my name with my authority

behold his sway observe his rule
brother of your order friar
habit friar's robes
moe more

FRIAR   It rested in your grace
        To unloose this tied-up justice when you pleased,
        And it in you more dreadful would have seemed
        Than in Lord Angelo.

DUKE   I do fear, too dreadful.   35
        Sith 'twas my fault to give the people scope,
        'Twould be my tyranny to strike and gall them
        For what I bid them do: for we bid this be done
        When evil deeds have their permissive pass
        And not the punishment. Therefore indeed, my father,   40
        I have on Angelo imposed the office,
        Who may in th'ambush of my name strike home,
        And yet my nature never in the fight
        To do in slander. And to behold his sway
        I will, as 'twere a brother of your order,   45
        Visit both prince and people. Therefore I prithee
        Supply me with the habit, and instruct me
        How I may formally in person bear
        Like a true friar. Moe reasons for this action
        At our more leisure shall I render you;   50
        Only this one: Lord Angelo is precise,
        Stands at a guard with envy, scarce confesses
        That his blood flows, or that his appetite
        Is more to bread than stone. Hence shall we see,
        If power change purpose, what our seemers be.   55

Exeunt

Isabella tells Francisca that she would welcome even more restrictions upon the order of nuns she is about to enter. Lucio informs Isabella of Claudio's imprisonment.

1 First sight of Isabella (in small groups)

Every director, and every actress who plays Isabella, gives a great deal of thought to how she should first appear. What should be the audience's first sight of her? Talk together about the following:

- What is she wearing – and why?
- How does she speak her first four lines?
- Why does she wish for 'a more strict restraint'? (the Poor Clares were already a very strict order of nuns)
- How do her first four lines link her with Angelo?
- How do they link her with Claudio?

Write up your conclusions.

2 Should the audience laugh? (in small groups)

Francisca the nun has only these few lines. As a director of the play, would you want to make the audience laugh when she tells the rules of the convent (lines 7–14)? Try different ways of speaking these lines to find what audience response you wish to evoke (for example, laugh, smile, accept seriously, and so on).

3 Lucio and Isabella – sacred and profane? (in pairs)

To gain an initial impression of how Lucio and Isabella talk to each other, take a part each and read through to the end of the scene.

- Pick out two lines that you think are 'typical' of Lucio.
- Pick out two lines 'typical' of Isabella.
- Make up two lists of five or six words each that express your view of the characters of Lucio and Isabella at this point in the play.

---

votarists of Saint Clare a strict order of nuns founded by St Francis of Assisi and St Clare in 1212. They wear white habits and follow a life of poverty, service and contemplation.

unsworn not fully a nun, not having sworn the vows
stead help
novice an unsworn nun, yet to take her vows
weary boring

ACT 1   SCENE 4
Vienna   The Convent of Saint Clare

Enter ISABELLA *and* FRANCISCA *a nun*

ISABELLA And have you nuns no farther privileges?
NUN Are not these large enough?
ISABELLA Yes, truly; I speak not as desiring more,
      But rather wishing a more strict restraint
      Upon the sisterhood, the votarists of Saint Clare.   5
LUCIO (*Within*) Ho? Peace be in this place.
ISABELLA   Who's that which calls?
NUN It is a man's voice. Gentle Isabella,
      Turn you the key and know his business of him.
      You may, I may not; you are yet unsworn:
      When you have vowed, you must not speak with men   10
      But in the presence of the prioress;
      Then if you speak you must not show your face,
      Or if you show your face you must not speak.
      He calls again: I pray you answer him. [*Stands aside*]
ISABELLA Peace and prosperity. Who is't that calls?   15

[Enter LUCIO*]*

LUCIO Hail virgin, if you be – as those cheek-roses
      Proclaim you are no less – can you so stead me
      As bring me to the sight of Isabella,
      A novice of this place and the fair sister
      To her unhappy brother Claudio?   20
ISABELLA Why 'her unhappy brother'? Let me ask,
      The rather for I now must make you know
      I am that Isabella, and his sister.
LUCIO Gentle and fair: your brother kindly greets you.
      Not to be weary with you, he's in prison.   25

Lucio, vowing to speak truthfully to Isabella, tells her that Claudio has made Juliet pregnant. He also describes the Duke's strange absence and Angelo's strict character.

1 How serious is Lucio? (in pairs)

After Isabella's reproof 'make me not your story', Lucio seems to become serious. But is he only seeming to be so? Read lines 30–44 aloud and talk together about whether you think he's genuinely serious or whether his tone is still mocking. In particular, decide whether you think he really does regard Isabella as 'a thing enskied and sainted'.

2 Shakespeare's ornithology

Shakespeare also uses the image of the lapwing in *The Comedy of Errors* and *Much Ado About Nothing*. Lucio's description of his own character as a lapwing (lines 32–3) echoes a major theme of the play: deceit. To lure intruders away from its nest, the lapwing feigns distress some distance away. Who else plays the lapwing ('Tongue far from heart') in Lucio's lines 50–61?

3 More about Angelo (in groups of three)

It is very difficult to be quite sure if Lucio ever tells the truth. None the less, his description of Angelo (lines 57–61) adds to the impression of Angelo as a man who has overcome his emotions and sexual desires. But this is the description given to Isabella, a young woman about to become a nun. How would Lucio describe Angelo to the two Gentlemen? Improvise!

---

make me not your story don't joke with me
enskied heavenly
renouncement decision to become a nun (and renounce the world)
Fewness and truth briefly and truly

seedness sown seed
bare fallow barren earth
teeming foison abundant harvest
tilth and husbandry cultivation
bore . . . action promised us military service
rebate reduce, dull

ISABELLA Woe me! For what?

LUCIO For that which, if myself might be his judge,
        He should receive his punishment in thanks:
        He hath got his friend with child.

ISABELLA Sir, make me not your story.

LUCIO   'Tis true.   30
        I would not, though 'tis my familiar sin
        With maids to seem the lapwing, and to jest
        Tongue far from heart, play with all virgins so.
        I hold you as a thing enskied and sainted,
        By your renouncement an immortal spirit,   35
        And to be talked with in sincerity
        As with a saint.

ISABELLA You do blaspheme the good in mocking me.

LUCIO Do not believe it. Fewness and truth, 'tis thus:
        Your brother and his lover have embraced;   40
        As those that feed grow full, as blossoming time
        That from the seedness the bare fallow brings
        To teeming foison, even so her plenteous womb
        Expresseth his full tilth and husbandry.

ISABELLA Someone with child by him? My cousin Juliet?   45

LUCIO Is she your cousin?

ISABELLA Adoptedly, as schoolmaids change their names
        By vain though apt affection.

LUCIO   She it is.

ISABELLA O, let him marry her.

LUCIO   This is the point.
        The Duke is very strangely gone from hence;   50
        Bore many gentlemen, myself being one,
        In hand and hope of action: but we do learn,
        By those that know the very nerves of state,
        His givings-out were of an infinite distance
        From his true meant design. Upon his place,   55
        And with full line of his authority,
        Governs Lord Angelo, a man whose blood
        Is very snow-broth; one who never feels
        The wanton stings and motions of the sense,
        But doth rebate and blunt his natural edge   60
        With profits of the mind: study and fast.

Lucio tells that Angelo has revived the old morality law, arrested Claudio, and intends to execute him. He asks Isabella to petition Angelo for Claudio's life. After some hesitation she agrees.

---

1 Absent scenes (in small groups)

Shakespeare often leaves gaps for imaginative filling-in.

- 'Has censured him already.' Role-play the trial of Claudio (line 72).
- Role-play the meeting between Isabella and the Mother Superior of the Convent (lines 86–7). As nun and novice, the Mother and Isabella may experience difficulty in finding language to talk together about what's going on (but they might not!).

2 Young women can get anything from men – or can they?

Do you think that what Claudio says about men and young women in lines 80–3 is really true? Or is it sexist stereotyping?

3 Parallels: private to public (in groups of four)

This demanding but rewarding activity identifies a similarity between Isabella and Angelo. Both are propelled from private life into public action by the demand or entreaty of another.

Take lines 68–90 opposite and lines 42–75 in Scene 1. Make a selection from each set of lines to construct a scene in which the two pairs of characters (Duke/Angelo, Lucio/Isabella) mirror each other's actions as they speak. Don't be afraid to repeat or cut lines.

4 Who's who? (in groups of five to seven)

Try 'pointing' your way through lines 62–90. As one person slowly reads all the lines, everyone else points to each person mentioned (for example, by name, or as 'he' or 'them', and so on). It sounds complicated, but you'll find you pick it up quickly. It will prove helpful to your understanding.

---

use sexual licence
statute law
my pith of business the essence or core of my story
censured sentenced

Assay employ
petitions pleas, requests
would owe them would wish to have

He, to give fear to use and liberty,
Which have for long run by the hideous law
As mice by lions, hath picked out an Act
Under whose heavy sense your brother's life   65
Falls into forfeit. He arrests him on it,
And follows close the rigour of the statute
To make him an example. All hope is gone,
Unless you have the grace by your fair prayer
To soften Angelo. And that's my pith of business   70
'Twixt you and your poor brother.
ISABELLA   Doth he so
        Seek his life?
LUCIO   Has censured him already,
        And, as I hear, the provost hath a warrant
        For's execution.
ISABELLA   Alas! What poor
        Ability's in me to do him good?   75
LUCIO Assay the power you have.
ISABELLA   My power? Alas, I doubt.
LUCIO Our doubts are traitors
        And makes us lose the good we oft might win,
        By fearing to attempt. Go to Lord Angelo
        And let him learn to know, when maidens sue   80
        Men give like gods, but when they weep and kneel
        All their petitions are as freely theirs
        As they themselves would owe them.
ISABELLA I'll see what I can do.
LUCIO But speedily.
ISABELLA   I will about it straight;   85
        No longer staying but to give the Mother
        Notice of my affair. I humbly thank you.
        Commend me to my brother: soon at night
        I'll send him certain word of my success.
LUCIO I take my leave of you.
ISABELLA   Good sir, adieu.   90
                                        Exeunt

Looking back at Act 1
Activities for groups or individuals

1 What's happened so far? Headlines

Imagine you are a newspaper sub-editor. Your job is to write brief, memorable headlines for each of the four scenes in Act 1. Make your four headlines as accurate as possible. Try to use some of Shakespeare's own words.

2 Make the action flow

Today, Shakespeare productions flow virtually without break from scene to scene. The four scenes of Act 1 are set in the Duke's palace, a street, Friar Thomas's monastery, and the convent of Saint Clare. Design a simple stage set that clearly specifies each place, yet enables the action to flow smoothly. Include notes suggesting how music, lighting and simple props can help indicate a change of scene.

3 Write the documents

Authority and law-enforcement in Vienna is backed up by legal documents. The written word has great power. Draw up one or more of the following legal documents that are crucial to Act 1. Use an appropriate style of language in each case.

- The commissions: delegating authority to Angelo and Escalus (Scene 1 lines 13, 17–21 and 43–6).
- The proclamation: ordering the closure of Vienna's brothels (Scene 2 line 80).
- The Act: under which Claudio is condemned (Scene 2 lines 147–51).
- The warrant: ordering the Provost to arrest and execute Claudio (Scene 4 lines 73–4).

4 Characters – early impressions

Consider in turn each character who has appeared in Act 1. Using the evidence from the script:
a say how each regards the opposite sex
b describe your current impression of each.

Check the accuracy of your judgements as you read on.

5 Change the genre: film or novel

- Imagine you are directing a film of *Measure for Measure*. Draw a storyboard (a set of pictures) to cover the first act.
- You are a famous novelist about to write your latest novel, inspired by *Measure for Measure*. Write Chapter 1 based on Act 1.

6 What historical period?

In which historical period would you set the play – and why? Design a costume for one or two characters to fit the period.

7 Bankside brothels

The Swan   The Lion   The Ship   The Hart   The Castle

THE STEWES

RIVER THAMES

In Shakespeare's time, Bankside, across the Thames from the City of London, contained many brothels. Shakespeare probably passed them daily on his way to work at the Globe. Although the Puritans raged against such open displays of sexuality, many powerful people profited from prostitution. The Lord Chamberlain, the Bishop of Winchester and some theatre-owners all owned property leased for brothels. Religious arguments were used to justify prostitution: 'suppress prostitution and capricious lusts will overthrow society' (St Augustine); 'Prostitution in the towns is like the cesspool [sewage pit] in the palace: take away the cesspool and the palace will become an unclean and evil-smelling place' (St Thomas Aquinas).

Organise a class debate (or write your own argument) for or against legal brothels. Make *Measure for Measure* your starting and finishing points.

Angelo insists that the law must not be neglected. Escalus urges leniency, asking Angelo if he too has not been sexually tempted. Angelo dismisses Escalus's plea; justice must be seen to be done.

1 Guilty judges (in pairs)

To gain a sense of the difference between Angelo and Escalus, read through lines 1–31 twice, changing roles. Then try one or more of the following:

- Escalus's appeal? One person reads aloud lines 8–16. The other echoes every 'you' or 'your'. Repeat this activity, then discuss whether Escalus makes a strong argument or an emotional appeal.
- Angelo's argument? Angelo acknowledges that juries may contain people who have committed undetected offences. He argues that that is no reason for not punishing known offenders. Talk together about the strength of Angelo's argument against Escalus.
- What do lines 1–31 reveal about the different personalities of Escalus and Angelo?

2 'A scarecrow of the law'

Draw the image that Angelo's first four lines call up in your imagination. Add as much detail as possible, based on the lines.

3 Biblical echoes?

'Judge not that ye be not judged' (St Matthew)
'Cast out the beam in your own eye' (St Luke) [beam = plank, obstruction]
'Let him that is without guilt cast the first stone' (St John)

Shakespeare would often have heard such biblical quotations in church. Can you find echoes of them opposite?

---

fear frighten
keen thoughtful, sharp
fall destroy (like cutting down a tree)
blood passion
censure condemn

what knows who knows
pregnant obvious
The jewel ... of it we can take account only of what we see or know

ACT 2   SCENE 1
Vienna   The law courts

Enter ANGELO, ESCALUS, and SERVANTS, and a JUSTICE

ANGELO   We must not make a scarecrow of the law,
   Setting it up to fear the birds of prey,
   And let it keep one shape till custom make it
   Their perch and not their terror.
ESCALUS   Ay, but yet
   Let us be keen, and rather cut a little   5
   Than fall and bruise to death. Alas, this gentleman
   Whom I would save had a most noble father.
   Let but your honour know,
   Whom I believe to be most strait in virtue,
   That in the working of your own affections,   10
   Had time cohered with place, or place with wishing,
   Or that the resolute acting of your blood
   Could have attained th'effect of your own purpose,
   Whether you had not sometime in your life
   Erred in this point which now you censure him,   15
   And pulled the law upon you.
ANGELO   'Tis one thing to be tempted, Escalus,
   Another thing to fall. I not deny
   The jury passing on the prisoner's life
   May in the sworn twelve have a thief or two   20
   Guiltier than him they try: what's open made to justice,
   That justice seizes. What knows the laws
   That thieves do pass on thieves? 'Tis very pregnant,
   The jewel that we find, we stoop and take't,
   Because we see it; but what we do not see   25
   We tread upon and never think of it.

Angelo says that if he offended like Claudio, he should also be executed. He orders Claudio's death at nine the next morning. Elbow brings in Pompey and Froth for judgement.

1 'And nothing come in partial' (in small groups)

Angelo (line 31) argues that the law should not take account of particular circumstances. But don't circumstances alter cases?

Debate whether greater justice results if the law is always strictly applied, regardless of the particular considerations of each individual case.

2 Advice required

The extent of Angelo's mercy: Angelo is prepared to grant Claudio the opportunity to confess his sins (lines 35–6) to prepare him for death. The actor playing Angelo asks you for advice on how to speak the lines 'because it seems to be a chink in Angelo's armour'. What advice do you offer?

Escalus's forgiveness: Escalus's lines 37–40 are a rhymed generalisation (sententiae) about forgiveness and law-breaking. Some people get away with many offences (line 39), but some are sentenced for their very first offence (line 40). Does Escalus say these lines to Angelo, to the audience, or to whom? Advise the actor, with reasons.

3 Comic business? (in groups of five)

With the entry of Elbow and Pompey, the mood shifts to comedy. To gain an initial impression of how this scene illuminates the play, read through lines 41–235 as Angelo, Escalus, Elbow, Pompey and Froth.

4 'Precise villains' (in pairs)

Later in the play, Angelo will be described as 'precise'. Show your partner how you think a precise person behaves.

For because
censure condemn
nothing come in partial no
  personal favours given
confessor priest

utmost of his pilgrimage end of
  his life's journey
use their abuses in common
  houses fornicate in brothels
out at elbow speechless (or stupid,
  or raggedly dressed)

You may not so extenuate his offence
For I have had such faults; but rather tell me,
When I that censure him do so offend,
Let mine own judgement pattern out my death   30
And nothing come in partial. Sir, he must die.

Enter PROVOST

ESCALUS Be it as your wisdom will.
ANGELO   Where is the provost?
PROVOST Here, if it like your honour.
ANGELO   See that Claudio
Be executed by nine tomorrow morning.
Bring him his confessor, let him be prepared,   35
For that's the utmost of his pilgrimage.

                                         [*Exit Provost*]
ESCALUS Well, heaven forgive him, and forgive us all.
Some rise by sin and some by virtue fall,
Some run from breaks of ice and answer none,
And some condemnèd for a fault alone.   40

Enter ELBOW [*and*] OFFICERS [*with*] FROTH [*and*] POMPEY

ELBOW Come, bring them away. If these be good people in a
commonweal, that do nothing but use their abuses in common
houses, I know no law. Bring them away.
ANGELO How now, sir, what's your name, and what's the matter?
ELBOW If it please your honour, I am the poor Duke's constable, and   45
my name is Elbow. I do lean upon justice, sir, and do bring in
here, before your good honour, two notorious benefactors.
ANGELO Benefactors? Well, what benefactors are they? Are they not
malefactors?
ELBOW If it please your honour, I know not well what they are: but   50
precise villains they are, that I am sure of, and void of all
profanation in the world that good Christians ought to have.
ESCALUS This comes off well: here's a wise officer.
ANGELO Go to. What quality are they of? Elbow is your name? Why
dost thou not speak, Elbow?   55
POMPEY He cannot, sir: he's out at elbow.

Elbow, muddling his words, implies that his wife has been compromised by Pompey. Pompey embarks on a long and involved story.

---

1 Elbow mangles the language (in pairs)

Shakespeare seems to have had a thing about constables. In *Much Ado About Nothing* another comic constable, Dogberry, mangles his words with the same careless unconcern. Both Elbow and Dogberry are like Mrs Malaprop in Sheridan's play *The Rivals* (1775). She gave us the word 'malapropism': mistaking one word for another (for example, 'detest' for 'respect').

- Read aloud all Elbow's lines, emphasising all his malapropisms. He begins (line 47) with 'benefactors' when he means 'malefactors'.
- Talk together about how the other characters on stage might respond to Elbow's language mistakes. Notice that Escalus comments directly on them at line 80.

2 Red herrings (in groups of four or five)

Pompey runs rings round everyone with his convoluted tale. He mimics formal and precise judicial language, and he deliberately sets out to confuse. He is also probably using much sexual innuendo that would have made Shakespeare's audiences laugh. Many of his expressions had sexual implications at the time: 'stewed prunes', 'dish', 'china', 'pin', 'point', 'two', 'stones'.

Act out this court scene with Pompey making as much as he can of the power of language to confuse. If he behaves like a barrister in court, it adds to the fun. Think carefully about how Angelo reacts as he listens.

---

tapster barman
parcel bawd part-time pimp (prostitute's assistant)
house/hot-house brothel

cardinally carnally (another Elbow malapropism)
stewed prunes a favourite dish in brothels

ANGELO What are you, sir?

ELBOW He, sir? A tapster, sir, parcel bawd, one that serves a bad
woman, whose house, sir, was, as they say, plucked down in the
suburbs; and now she professes a hot-house; which I think is a   60
very ill house too.

ESCALUS How know you that?

ELBOW My wife, sir, whom I detest before heaven and your honour –

ESCALUS How? Thy wife?

ELBOW Ay, sir: whom I thank heaven is an honest woman –   65

ESCALUS Dost thou detest her therefore?

ELBOW I say, sir, I will detest myself also, as well as she, that this
house, if it be not a bawd's house, it is pity of her life, for it is a
naughty house.

ESCALUS How dost thou know that, constable?   70

ELBOW Marry, sir, by my wife, who, if she had been a woman
cardinally given, might have been accused in fornication,
adultery, and all uncleanliness there.

ESCALUS By the woman's means?

ELBOW Ay, sir, by Mistress Overdone's means. But as she spit in his   75
face, so she defied him.

POMPEY Sir, if it please your honour, this is not so.

ELBOW Prove it before these varlets here, thou honourable man,
prove it!

ESCALUS Do you hear how he misplaces?   80

POMPEY Sir, she came in great with child; and longing, saving your
honours' reverence, for stewed prunes. Sir, we had but two in
the house, which at that very distant time stood, as it were, in a
fruit dish, a dish of some three pence; your honours have seen
such dishes, they are not china dishes, but very good dishes –   85

ESCALUS Go to, go to: no matter for the dish, sir.

POMPEY No indeed, sir, not of a pin; you are therein in the right –
but to the point: as I say, this Mistress Elbow, being, as I say,
with child, and being great-bellied, and longing, as I said, for
prunes, and having but two in the dish, as I said, Master Froth   90
here, this very man, having eaten the rest, as I said, and, as I say,
paying for them very honestly – for as you know, Master Froth, I
could not give you three pence again –

FROTH No indeed.

POMPEY Very well. You being then, if you be remembered, cracking   95
the stones of the foresaid prunes –

Pompey wearies the patience of Escalus and Angelo with his meandering story. Angelo leaves Escalus to judge the case. Pompey continues his tricks.

1 Who's who?

Pompey makes a point. Identify the characters and find a line opposite that you think is being spoken at this moment (Shakespeare Memorial Theatre, 1940).

2 More about Angelo

Does the puritanical Angelo make a joke at 118–19, or is he just exasperated?

What does his exit line (121) suggest about his judicial impartiality?

the thing you wot of 'you know what' (syphilis)
Hallowmas 1 November (All Saints' Day)

All-Hallond Eve 31 October (the eve of All Saints)

FROTH Ay, so I did indeed.

POMPEY Why, very well. I telling you then, if you be remembered, that such a one, and such a one, were past cure of the thing you wot of, unless they kept very good diet, as I told you –   100

FROTH All this is true.

POMPEY Why very well then –

ESCALUS Come, you are a tedious fool, to the purpose: what was done to Elbow's wife, that he hath cause to complain of? Come me to what was done to her.   105

POMPEY Sir, your honour cannot come to that yet.

ESCALUS No, sir, nor I mean it not.

POMPEY Sir, but you shall come to it, by your honour's leave; and I beseech you, look into Master Froth here, sir; a man of four score pound a year; whose father died at Hallowmas – was't not   110 at Hallowmas, Master Froth?

FROTH All-Hallond Eve.

POMPEY Why, very well: I hope here be truths. He, sir, sitting, as I say, in a lower chair, sir – 'twas in the Bunch of Grapes, where indeed you have a delight to sit, have you not?   115

FROTH I have so, because it is an open room, and good for winter.

POMPEY Why, very well then: I hope here be truths.

ANGELO This will last out a night in Russia
  When nights are longest there. I'll take my leave,
  And leave you to the hearing of the cause,   120
  Hoping you'll find good cause to whip them all.   *Exit*

ESCALUS I think no less: good morrow to your lordship.
  Now, sir, come on: what was done to Elbow's wife, once more?

POMPEY Once, sir? There was nothing done to her once.

ELBOW I beseech you, sir, ask him what this man did to my wife.   125

POMPEY I beseech your honour, ask me.

ESCALUS Well, sir, what did this gentleman to her?

POMPEY I beseech you, sir, look in this gentleman's face. Good Master Froth, look upon his honour; 'tis for a good purpose. Doth your honour mark his face?   130

ESCALUS Ay, sir, very well.

POMPEY Nay, I beseech you mark it well.

ESCALUS Well, I do so.

POMPEY Doth your honour see any harm in his face?

ESCALUS Why, no.   135

Elbow misunderstands 'respected' and flies into a rage at the thought that his wife is immoral. Escalus, amused, 'sentences' Pompey to continue his behaviour until Elbow discovers his offences. Elbow is delighted.

1 More 'seeming'

Escalus apparently agrees with Pompey's 'defence' of Froth that because Froth looks innocent (no 'harm in his face'), he must be innocent. What kind of justice is that? It ironically echoes the theme of deceit ('seeming') that runs through the play.

Do you think Escalus is serious when he agrees with Pompey?

2 Escalus joins in the fun

What does Escalus's 'sentence' (158–60) suggest to you about Escalus's personality – and Elbow's?

3 Froth – and Elbow's wife (in small groups)

Just what did Froth do to Elbow's wife?

- Discuss possible reasons why it is never revealed in the play.
- Improvise what might have happened.

4 Justice or Iniquity? (in pairs)

Escalus's line 148 refers both to the two stock characters in medieval Morality plays and to Elbow and Pompey. Balancing law versus vice is a major theme of the play, echoed in the language (see page 184).

- Invent a number of tableaux showing different ways of portraying Justice and Iniquity in opposition to each other.
- Design a book jacket with the title *Justice and Iniquity*.
- Justice and Iniquity are personifications (abstract qualities imagined as living persons). Draw a series of cartoons showing the babyhood, adolescence, maturity and old age of Justice and Iniquity.

---

be supposed upon a book swear upon the Bible
respected suspected (another Elbow malapropism)
caitiff rogue
Hannibal cannibal (who, like a pimp, trades in bodies)

battery physical assault
slander false verbal assault
tapster barman
by the last by the last husband (and the innuendo: sexually worn out)

POMPEY I'll be supposed upon a book, his face is the worst thing
  about him: good then: if his face be the worst thing about him,
  how could Master Froth do the constable's wife any harm? I
  would know that of your honour.

ESCALUS He's in the right, constable, what say you to it? 140

ELBOW First, and it like you, the house is a respected house; next,
  this is a respected fellow; and his mistress is a respected woman.

POMPEY By this hand, sir, his wife is a more respected person than
  any of us all.

ELBOW Varlet, thou liest! Thou liest, wicked varlet! The time is yet 145
  to come that she was ever respected with man, woman, or child.

POMPEY Sir, she was respected with him before he married with her.

ESCALUS Which is the wiser here, Justice or Iniquity? Is this true?

ELBOW Oh, thou caitiff! Oh, thou varlet! Oh, thou wicked Hannibal!
  I respected with her, before I was married to her? If ever I was 150
  respected with her, or she with me, let not your worship think me
  the poor Duke's officer! Prove this, thou wicked Hannibal, or I'll
  have mine action of battery on thee.

ESCALUS If he took you a box o'th'ear, you might have your action of
  slander too. 155

ELBOW Marry, I thank your good worship for it. What is't your
  worship's pleasure I shall do with this wicked caitiff?

ESCALUS Truly, officer, because he hath some offences in him that
  thou wouldst discover, if thou couldst, let him continue in his
  courses till thou knowst what they are. 160

ELBOW Marry, I thank your worship for it. Thou seest, thou wicked
  varlet, now, what's come upon thee. Thou art to continue, now,
  thou varlet, thou art to continue.

ESCALUS Where were you born, friend?

FROTH Here in Vienna, sir. 165

ESCALUS Are you of four score pounds a year?

FROTH Yes, and't please you, sir.

ESCALUS So. [To Pompey] What trade are you of, sir?

POMPEY A tapster, a poor widow's tapster.

ESCALUS Your mistress' name? 170

POMPEY Mistress Overdone.

ESCALUS Hath she had any more than one husband?

POMPEY Nine, sir: Overdone by the last.

Escalus dismisses Froth with a warning. He threatens Pompey with punishment for pimping. Pompey replies that if all prostitutes and clients were executed, Vienna would be practically empty.

1 Who is Froth? (in small groups)

Froth appears only in this scene, and has only nine lines. Speak them aloud to each other several times, then talk together about what kind of character he is. He is a man of some wealth (£80 a year was a considerable sum). So how did he get caught up with Pompey and the others? Tell his story. Suggest appropriate dress, manner and actions.

2 Escalus's jokes

In the 1988 Royal Shakespeare Company production, the director ensured that Escalus's jokes fell flat. They were mockingly regarded with derision or incredulity by Pompey and his friends on stage.

As a director, how would you want the on-stage characters to behave at Escalus's jokes at 175–6 and 186–7? Your suggestions will depend on how you envisage Pompey and his friends.

'Pompey the Great': Escalus refers not only to the historical Pompey (a Roman general defeated by Julius Caesar) but to the padded breeches Pompey wore in the original productions. One of Shakespeare's contemporaries condemned the excesses of dress of the time: 'we men do seem to bestowe most cost upon our arses'.

draw cheat, deceive or dismember
taphouse inn
drawn enticed, cheated or drawn like beer from a barrel
colour disguise
the trade prostitution

geld and splay castrate
take order for take care of
drabs/knaves prostitutes and their clients
pretty orders new laws
three pence a bay very cheaply

ESCALUS Nine? Come hither to me, Master Froth. Master Froth, I
would not have you acquainted with tapsters; they will draw you,   175
Master Froth, and you will hang them. Get you gone, and let me
hear no more of you.

FROTH I thank your worship. For mine own part, I never come into
any room in a taphouse, but I am drawn in.

ESCALUS Well, no more of it, Master Froth. Farewell.   180

[*Exit Froth*]

Come you hither to me, Master Tapster. What's your name,
Master Tapster?

POMPEY Pompey.

ESCALUS What else?

POMPEY Bum, sir.   185

ESCALUS Troth, and your bum is the greatest thing about you, so
that in the beastliest sense you are Pompey the Great. Pompey,
you are partly a bawd, Pompey, howsoever you colour it in being
a tapster, are you not? Come, tell me true, it shall be the better
for you.   190

POMPEY Truly, sir, I am a poor fellow that would live.

ESCALUS How would you live, Pompey? By being a bawd? What do
you think of the trade, Pompey? Is it a lawful trade?

POMPEY If the law would allow it, sir.

ESCALUS But the law will not allow it, Pompey; nor it shall not be   195
allowed in Vienna.

POMPEY Does your worship mean to geld and splay all the youth of
the city?

ESCALUS No, Pompey.

POMPEY Truly, sir, in my poor opinion they will to't then. If your   200
worship will take order for the drabs and the knaves, you need
not to fear the bawds.

ESCALUS There is pretty orders beginning, I can tell you: it is but
heading and hanging.

POMPEY If you head and hang all that offend that way but for ten   205
year together, you'll be glad to give out a commission for more
heads. If this law hold in Vienna ten year, I'll rent the fairest
house in it after three pence a bay. If you live to see this come to
pass, say Pompey told you so.

Escalus dismisses Pompey, warning him that he will be whipped next time. Pompey is undismayed. Escalus questions Elbow about his office as constable, then leaves with a word of sorrow for Claudio.

1 How did Elbow get the job?

Elbow gets the job as constable because no one else wants to do it (lines 230–1). Escalus wishes to identify others who could serve as constable (line 232). Use the library to find out all you can about the Watch (the police) in Shakespeare's time. Then write two versions of how Elbow was appointed constable: one by Elbow, one by his neighbour who doesn't want the job.

2 What's in a name? (in pairs)

Escalus's jokes on the appropriateness of Pompey Bum's name. Shakespeare, like many other writers (particularly Charles Dickens), sometimes gave his characters names that suggest their personalities or dramatic function. Here are a few of the interpretations that have been suggested:

Escalus = scales of justice Vincentio = victor
Angelo = bad angel Lucio = Lucifer, the Devil.

Research into the appropriateness (or inappropriateness) of the names of other characters in the play (some names will not have symbolic meaning). Compare your findings with other students'.

3 The Justice? (in groups of four)

This is the Justice's only appearance. Does he add anything to the play? Argue for and against cutting him out of your production.

4 A final couplet

Escalus ends (lines 244–5) with a rhyming couplet. Has he changed his view about mercy from the one he expressed in lines 4–7?

Pompey/Caesar Pompey was a Roman general defeated by Julius Caesar
requital of exchange for
shrewd stern
carman carter

jade broken-down horse (or prostitute)
ward district
sufficient competent
Pardon . . . woe mercy results in later sorrow (see 2.2.103–7)

ESCALUS Thank you, good Pompey; and in requital of your   210
prophecy, hark you: I advise you, let me not find you before me
again upon any complaint whatsoever; no, not for dwelling where
you do. If I do, Pompey, I shall beat you to your tent, and prove a
shrewd Caesar to you: in plain dealing, Pompey, I shall have you
whipped. So for this time, Pompey, fare you well.   215
POMPEY I thank your worship for your good counsel; [*Aside*] but I
shall follow it as the flesh and fortune shall better determine.
    Whip me? No, no, let carman whip his jade,
    The valiant heart's not whipped out of his trade.   *Exit*
ESCALUS Come hither to me, Master Elbow, come hither, Master   220
Constable. How long have you been in this place of constable?
ELBOW Seven year, and a half, sir.
ESCALUS I thought, by the readiness in the office, you had continued
in it some time. You say seven years together?
ELBOW And a half, sir.   225
ESCALUS Alas, it hath been great pains to you: they do you wrong to
put you so oft upon't. Are there not men in your ward sufficient
to serve it?
ELBOW Faith, sir, few of any wit in such matters. As they are chosen,
they are glad to choose me for them; I do it for some piece of   230
money, and go through with all.
ESCALUS Look you bring me in the names of some six or seven, the
most sufficient of your parish.
ELBOW To your worship's house, sir?
ESCALUS To my house. Fare you well.   235
                                   [*Exit Elbow*]
    What's a clock, think you?
JUSTICE Eleven, sir.
ESCALUS I pray you home to dinner with me.
JUSTICE I humbly thank you.
ESCALUS It grieves me for the death of Claudio,   240
    But there's no remedy.
JUSTICE Lord Angelo is severe.
ESCALUS It is but needful.
    Mercy is not itself that oft looks so,
    Pardon is still the nurse of second woe.   245
  But yet, poor Claudio; there is no remedy. Come sir.
                                 Exeunt

The Provost hopes that Claudio will be reprieved, but Angelo orders him to carry out the death sentence or be dismissed. Angelo also orders that Juliet be sent away.

1 What cause?

Angelo is trying a case. What might it be? Write down three likely offences that Angelo is trying as he strives to clean up Vienna. Suggest what sentences he hands out in each case.

2 Status and character (in groups of three)

Read lines 1–26 three times, so that each person takes each role. From these lines alone, what can you deduce about the relative status and personalities of the three characters? It will help if you identify all the commands that are given, and notice who makes them.

3 Disposing of Juliet

'Two of the most terrifying lines in the play', wrote one student about Angelo's lines 17–18. If you were marking her essay, what comments would you make on her claim?

Angelo, Royal Shakespeare Company, 1987. Find descriptions of Angelo in the script which would be suitable captions to this picture.

---

hearing of a cause trying a case
All sects Every society
in a dream unintentionally
doom sentence

you shall well be spared you are not indispensable
groaning in labour
hour time to give birth

ACT 2 SCENE 2
A room in Angelo's house

Enter PROVOST *and a* SERVANT

SERVANT He's hearing of a cause, he will come straight,
    I'll tell him of you.
PROVOST   Pray you do.

                                  [*Exit Servant*]
                           I'll know
    His pleasure, may be he will relent. Alas,
    He hath but as offended in a dream.
    All sects, all ages smack of this vice, and he   5
    To die for't?

Enter ANGELO

ANGELO   Now what's the matter, provost?
PROVOST Is it your will Claudio shall die tomorrow?
ANGELO Did not I tell thee yea? Hadst thou not order?
    Why dost thou ask again?
PROVOST   Lest I might be too rash:
    Under your good correction, I have seen   10
    When, after execution, judgement hath
    Repented o'er his doom.
ANGELO   Go to; let that be mine.
    Do you your office, or give up your place,
    And you shall well be spared.
PROVOST I crave your honour's pardon: 15
    What shall be done, sir, with the groaning Juliet?
    She's very near her hour.
ANGELO   Dispose of her
    To some more fitter place, and that with speed.

[*Enter* SERVANT]

SERVANT Here is the sister of the man condemned,
    Desires access to you.

Angelo orders modest provision for Juliet. Isabella, saying that she loathes fornication, asks Angelo none the less to spare Claudio. He is unmoved, but Lucio urges Isabella to plead again more strongly.

1 Read through the scene (in groups of three)

To gain a first impression of the scene, take parts (one person reads both Lucio and the Provost) and read through lines 26–166). Then try one or more of the activities that follow.

2 'Stay a little while' (in pairs)

Angelo asks the Provost to stay to hear his conversation with Isabella. But why? Suggest three possible reasons.

3 Who stands? Who sits? (in small groups)

Talk together about how you would begin to stage this encounter between Angelo and Isabella. Write notes, keyed to particular lines, to help the actors with movement and gesture.

4 Isabella: four moods?

Consider each of Isabella's four speeches opposite. Identify the mood or tone in which you think each should be spoken. To help you decide appropriate moods, select words in each speech that you think she would particularly emphasise.

Do the same with each speech of Angelo's. Does his tone vary from speech to speech?

5 'Let it be his fault . . .' (in pairs)

Angelo rejects Isabella's entreaty to condemn the crime, not Claudio. He argues it would make his task as judge meaningless if he did not punish wrongdoers. Discuss together whether you think there is any logic or justice in Isabella's plea in lines 36–7.

---

sisterhood order of nuns
fornicatress Juliet (person who has had illegal sex)
Save God save
suit plea
cipher of a function a meaningless role

fine punish/punishment
in record on the statute books (in law)
pin a tiny thing (Lucio is criticising Isabella's lack of forceful argument)

ANGELO   Hath he a sister?   20
PROVOST Ay, my good lord, a very virtuous maid,
      And to be shortly of a sisterhood,
      If not already.
ANGELO   Well. Let her be admitted.
                            [Exit Servant]
      See you the fornicatress be removed.
      Let her have needful, but not lavish, means.   25
      There shall be order for't.

Enter LUCIO *and* ISABELLA

PROVOST   Save your honour. *[Going]*
ANGELO Stay a little while. *[To Isabella]* Y'are welcome: what's your
      will?
ISABELLA I am a woeful suitor to your honour,
      Please but your honour hear me.
ANGELO   Well; what's your suit?
ISABELLA There is a vice that most I do abhor,   30
      And most desire should meet the blow of justice;
      For which I would not plead, but that I must,
      For which I must not plead, but that I am
      At war 'twixt will and will not.
ANGELO   Well; the matter?
ISABELLA I have a brother is condemned to die.   35
      I do beseech you, let it be his fault,
      And not my brother.
PROVOST *[Aside]*   Heaven give thee moving graces!
ANGELO Condemn the fault, and not the actor of it?
      Why, every fault's condemned ere it be done.
      Mine were the very cipher of a function   40
      To fine the faults, whose fine stands in record,
      And let go by the actor.
ISABELLA   Oh just but severe law:
      I had a brother then. Heaven keep your honour. *[Going]*
LUCIO *[To Isabella]* Give't not o'er so: to him again, entreat him,
      Kneel down before him, hang upon his gown.   45
      You are too cold. If you should need a pin,
      You could not with more tame a tongue desire it:
      To him, I say.

Angelo adamantly refuses to change his sentence as Isabella makes ever stronger pleas for mercy for Claudio.

---

1 Surround Angelo! (in groups of six to seven)

One person is Angelo, all the others are Isabella.

Isabellas: your task is to convince Angelo! Surround him and speak your lines 60–81 in turn, each person reading up to a punctuation mark, then handing on to the next person. Angelo must turn to face each 'Isabella' who speaks.

Experiment with different styles of delivering Isabella's words (angrily, reasonably, thoughtfully, desperately, very fast, and so on). Also try different ways of speaking Angelo's lines attempting to dismiss Isabella.

2 The quality of mercy (in groups of four)

Mercy, says Isabella, is more fitting to people holding great authority than crowns, swords, staffs of office, or ceremonial robes.

Find a copy of *The Merchant of Venice* and read Portia's speech on mercy in Act 4. Make a powerful presentation on 'Mercy', using Portia's lines and lines 60–4, 75–81 opposite. Try 'inter-cutting' the speeches, and don't be afraid to repeat lines.

3 Men are sinners, God is merciful (in pairs)

Lines 75–81 resonate with echoes of the Bible. They speak of God's forgiveness; of St Matthew's 'Judge not, that ye be not judged'; of redemption through the divine mercy of Jesus Christ; and of new life breathed into men by God.

Work out how the impact of Isabella's words might be heightened by her costume, gestures and expressions (and by props and the stage set).

---

remorse compassion, pity
longs belongs
deputed sword sword of justice (symbolising divine authority of kings as God's deputies)
marshal's truncheon army officer's baton

become enhance, or make fitting
potency power
he . . . took God (the One who judges everyone)

ISABELLA Must he needs die?
ANGELO   Maiden, no remedy.
ISABELLA Yes: I do think that you might pardon him,   50
     And neither heaven nor man grieve at the mercy.
ANGELO I will not do't.
ISABELLA   But can you if you would?
ANGELO Look what I will not, that I cannot do.
ISABELLA But might you do't, and do the world no wrong,
     If so your heart were touched with that remorse   55
     As mine is to him?
ANGELO   He's sentenced, 'tis too late.
LUCIO [To Isabella] You are too cold.
ISABELLA Too late? Why, no; I that do speak a word
     May call it again. Well, believe this:
     No ceremony that to great ones longs,   60
     Not the king's crown, nor the deputed sword,
     The marshal's truncheon, nor the judge's robe
     Become them with one half so good a grace
     As mercy does.
     If he had been as you, and you as he,   65
     You would have slipped like him, but he like you
     Would not have been so stern.
ANGELO   Pray you be gone.
ISABELLA I would to heaven I had your potency,
     And you were Isabel: should it then be thus?
     No. I would tell what 'twere to be a judge,   70
     And what a prisoner.
LUCIO [Aside] Ay, touch him, there's the vein.
ANGELO Your brother is a forfeit of the law,
     And you but waste your words.
ISABELLA   Alas, alas!
     Why all the souls that were, were forfeit once,   75
     And he that might the vantage best have took
     Found out the remedy. How would you be
     If he, which is the top of judgement, should
     But judge you as you are? Oh, think on that,
     And mercy then will breathe within your lips   80
     Like man new made.

49

Angelo says that the law, not he himself, condemns Claudio. Enforcing the law shows pity because it prevents future harm to others: Claudio must die. Isabella claims that such mighty use of power is tyranny.

1 Isabella's reasons versus Angelo's reasons
(in small groups)

Isabella makes four further arguments why Claudio should be spared:

a It's too soon, he's not prepared for death
b Many others have similarly offended
c Pity should be shown
d It's tyranny to condemn him to death.

In reply, Angelo gives three major reasons why Claudio must die:

a The law, not a person, condemns him (82)
b It acts as a deterrent to others (93–102)
c It protects innocent people later (103–7).

Put each set of arguments in order of priority as you see them. Who do you consider has the stronger set of reasons: Isabella or Angelo?

Take each reason in turn offered by Isabella and Angelo. Talk together about how strongly each applies (a) to Claudio's case, (b) to a murderer.

2 Tyranny (in small groups)

'Oh, it is excellent
To have a giant's strength, but it is tyrannous
To use it like a giant.'

Explore ways to show Isabella's vivid image as powerfully as you can, through tableau, drawing, story, finding contemporary examples, and so on (for example, in 1992 an ex-heavyweight boxing champion of the world was convicted of rape. In the 1930s dictator Joseph Stalin directed the murder of millions of his own citizens.)

---

kinsman relative
of season at the appropriate time
th'edict the law
glass crystal ball to foretell the future

Either now . . . conceived either already thought of, or evilly thought of later
successive degrees future growth
gall hurt

ANGELO   Be you content, fair maid,
          It is the law, not I, condemn your brother.
          Were he my kinsman, brother, or my son,
          It should be thus with him: he must die tomorrow.
ISABELLA Tomorrow? Oh, that's sudden! Spare him, spare him!   85
          He's not prepared for death. Even for our kitchens
          We kill the fowl of season: shall we serve heaven
          With less respect than we do minister
          To our gross selves? Good, good my lord, bethink you.
          Who is it that hath died for this offence?   90
          There's many have committed it.
LUCIO [*Aside*] Ay, well said.
ANGELO The law hath not been dead, though it hath slept.
          Those many had not dared to do that evil
          If the first that did th'edict infringe   95
          Had answered for his deed. Now 'tis awake,
          Takes note of what is done, and like a prophet
          Looks in a glass that shows what future evils –
          Either now, or by remissness new conceived,
          And so in progress to be hatched and born –   100
          Are now to have no successive degrees,
          But here they live to end.
ISABELLA   Yet show some pity.
ANGELO I show it most of all when I show justice;
          For then I pity those I do not know,
          Which a dismissed offence would after gall,   105
          And do him right, that answering one foul wrong
          Lives not to act another. Be satisfied.
          Your brother dies tomorrow. Be content.
ISABELLA So you must be the first that gives this sentence,
          And he, that suffers. Oh, it is excellent   110
          To have a giant's strength, but it is tyrannous
          To use it like a giant.
LUCIO [*Aside*] That's well said.

Isabella is powerfully scornful of man's arrogant use of authority. She again asks Angelo to search his heart to discover a similar vice to Claudio's. Angelo is sexually attracted and asks her to return tomorrow.

1 Arrogant authority (in small groups)

Isabella's onslaught on the arrogant use of authority (lines 109–45) is impassioned and scornful.

a Read the lines aloud in a variety of ways (sarcastically, angrily, rationally, mockingly, and so on) to discover appropriate tones.

b Contrasts: Isabella constantly weighs one thing (or person) against another. Each of her sentences contains one or more contrasts (antitheses) as she 'measures' Angelo against Claudio, having strength against using strength, and so on. Read her lines aloud and make a gesture to emphasise each of her 'weighing contrasts'.

c Tableau the simile 'like an angry ape / Plays such fantastic tricks before high heaven / As makes the angels weep' (lines 124–6).

d Direct it at Angelo! One person reads aloud lines 114–27. The others cry 'Angelo!' at the end of each line. Afterwards, discuss whether repeating 'Angelo!' heightens Isabella's sarcasm.

e Collect pictures (from newspapers, magazines) to illustrate 'man, proud man, / Dressed in a little brief authority'.

2 Angelo's aside

In lines 146–7 Angelo uses 'sense' to mean 'reason' (''tis such sense') and 'sensuality' ('my sense breeds with it'). How would you direct Angelo to show his growing sexual interest in Isabella during this scene? At what point do you think he first begins to desire her sexually?

Jove supreme Greek god
sulphurous bolt thunderbolt
unwedgeable unsplittable
glassy essence soul (reflection of God's image)
spleens (the spleen was thought to be the source of laughter)

with saints about religion
the less lower-status persons
choleric angry
Art avised o'that? do you know that?
skins the vice covers the sore with new skin

ISABELLA Could great men thunder
    As Jove himself does, Jove would ne'er be quiet,   115
    For every pelting, petty officer
    Would use his heaven for thunder –
    Nothing but thunder. Merciful heaven,
    Thou rather with thy sharp and sulphurous bolt
    Splits the unwedgeable and gnarlèd oak   120
    Than the soft myrtle; but man, proud man,
    Dressed in a little brief authority,
    Most ignorant of what he's most assured,
    His glassy essence, like an angry ape
    Plays such fantastic tricks before high heaven   125
    As makes the angels weep; who, with our spleens,
    Would all themselves laugh mortal.
LUCIO [Aside] Oh, to him, to him, wench, he will relent.
    He's coming: I perceive't.
PROVOST [Aside]   Pray heaven she win him!
ISABELLA We cannot weigh our brother with ourself.   130
    Great men may jest with saints: 'tis wit in them,
    But in the less foul profanation.
LUCIO [Aside] Thou'rt i'th'right, girl, more o'that!
ISABELLA That in the captain's but a choleric word
    Which in the soldier is flat blasphemy.   135
LUCIO [Aside] Art avised o'that? More on't.
ANGELO Why do you put these sayings upon me?
ISABELLA Because authority, though it err like others,
    Hath yet a kind of medicine in itself
    That skins the vice o'th'top. Go to your bosom,   140
    Knock there, and ask your heart what it doth know
    That's like my brother's fault. If it confess
    A natural guiltiness, such as is his,
    Let it not sound a thought upon your tongue
    Against my brother's life.   145
ANGELO [Aside] She speaks, and 'tis such sense
    That my sense breeds with it. [To Isabella] Fare you well.
ISABELLA Gentle my lord, turn back.
ANGELO I will bethink me. Come again tomorrow.

53

Isabella tells Angelo that his reward for mercy will be the prayers of nuns. Angelo commands her to visit him tomorrow. Left alone, he reveals his lust for Isabella. Her virtue makes him desire her.

---

1 Angelo's agitation (in pairs)

To catch the sense of Angelo's reeling mind, each partner takes a turn in reading lines 166–91. Read only to a punctuation mark, then hand on to your partner. Read as quickly as you can. If possible, move around the room as you read, changing direction frequently. Afterwards, discuss how your movement and way of speaking embody Angelo's feelings.

2 Prayers outweigh money

Not gold, but prayers, shall be Angelo's reward for sparing Claudio, says Isabella. Make an illustration to show that prayers are more worthwhile than money or jewels. Show as much detail from lines 154–60 as you can. Then make another illustration to show how, in line 163, Angelo's prayer crosses (conflicts with) Isabella's.

3 A puzzling image

Critics have long argued over the interpretation of lines 174–6. Work out a number of possible meanings and choose the one you prefer. 'Waste ground' may mean 'prostitutes'; 'evils' may mean 'privies' (lavatories); sanctuary may mean 'holy place' or Isabella; 'pitch' may mean 'thrown down', or 'put up', or 'blacken'.

4 Advise the actor

The actor playing Angelo seeks your advice. He says, 'Here's my problem. There are many difficult ideas and ambiguities in this speech. So how should I do it to provide the best dramatic experience for the audience?' What do you reply?

---

marred all else spoilt your argument otherwise
fond sickles . . . gold foolishly valued coins (shekels) of pure gold
stones jewels
rate worth, price
preserved souls nuns

nothing temporal only spiritual matters
tempter Isabella (or the Devil)
carrion rotten flesh, dead body
Corrupt . . . season rot in the sun
lightness immorality
raze destroy

ISABELLA Hark how I'll bribe you – good my lord, turn back.   150
ANGELO How? Bribe me?
ISABELLA Ay, with such gifts that heaven shall share with you.
LUCIO [*Aside*] You had marred all else.
ISABELLA Not with fond sickles of the tested gold,
     Or stones whose rate are either rich or poor   155
     As fancy values them; but with true prayers,
     That shall be up at heaven and enter there
     Ere sun rise – prayers from preservèd souls,
     From fasting maids whose minds are dedicate
     To nothing temporal.
ANGELO   Well; come to me tomorrow.   160
LUCIO [*To Isabella*] Go to. 'Tis well. Away.
ISABELLA Heaven keep your honour safe.
ANGELO [*Aside*]   Amen.
     For I am that way going to temptation
     Where prayers cross.
ISABELLA   At what hour tomorrow
     Shall I attend your lordship?
ANGELO   At any time 'fore noon.   165
ISABELLA Save your honour.
               [*Exeunt Isabella, Lucio and Provost*]
ANGELO   From thee: even from thy virtue.
     What's this? What's this? Is this her fault, or mine?
     The tempter or the tempted, who sins most, ha?
     Not she: nor doth she tempt: but it is I
     That, lying by the violet in the sun,   170
     Do as the carrion does, not as the flower,
     Corrupt with virtuous season. Can it be
     That modesty may more betray our sense
     Than woman's lightness? Having waste ground enough
     Shall we desire to raze the sanctuary   175
     And pitch our evils there? Oh fie, fie, fie,
     What dost thou or what art thou, Angelo?
     Dost thou desire her foully for those things
     That make her good? Oh, let her brother live:
     Thieves for their robbery have authority   180
     When judges steal themselves. What, do I love her
     That I desire to hear her speak again
     And feast upon her eyes? What is't I dream on?

Angelo is amazed at the strength of his desire for Isabella. Her virtue has tempted him into lust. In Scene 3 the disguised Duke visits the prison.

1 Answer Angelo's question (in small groups)

'Can it be/That modesty may more betray our sense/Than woman's lightness?' asks Angelo. He expresses this thought in six different ways in lines 166–91. Talk together about:

- Whether you think innocence and purity is more likely to prove attractive than open displays of sexuality. Is goodness more tempting than vice?
- Whether Angelo expresses a typical male viewpoint. What is a woman's point of view on this?

2 Fishing for saints (in small groups)

Find an active way of showing the image in lines 184–5.

3 Views of Angelo (in groups of six)

Take parts. One person, as a newspaper reporter, interviews Isabella, the Provost, Lucio, Claudio and Angelo at the end of Scene 2. Each is asked the same question: 'What is your view of Angelo at this moment?'

4 The Provost

What can you infer about the Provost's character from lines 9–15? Think of three or four adjectives that you feel describe his character.

5 Does the Duke forget his disguise?

The actor playing the Duke asks you: 'I have a problem with line 1. Does it mean I make a mistake as the Friar in the first few words, then recover?' What do you reply?

---

goad spur
strumpet prostitute
double false
fond foolishly in love
charity vow to do good deeds

blessed order brotherhood of friars
flaws passionate failings
got fathered

Oh cunning enemy that, to catch a saint,
With saints dost bait thy hook! Most dangerous   185
Is that temptation that doth goad us on
To sin in loving virtue. Never could the strumpet
With all her double vigour, art and nature,
Once stir my temper; but this virtuous maid
Subdues me quite. Ever till now   190
When men were fond, I smiled, and wondered how. *Exit*

ACT 2   SCENE 3
Vienna   The prison

Enter DUKE [disguised as a friar] *and* PROVOST

DUKE Hail to you, provost – so I think you are.
PROVOST I am the provost. What's your will, good friar?
DUKE Bound by my charity and my blessèd order
    I come to visit the afflicted spirits
    Here in the prison. Do me the common right   5
    To let me see them and to make me know
    The nature of their crimes, that I may minister
    To them accordingly.
PROVOST I would do more than that, if more were needful.

Enter JULIET

    Look, here comes one, a gentlewoman of mine,   10
    Who, falling in the flaws of her own youth,
    Hath blistered her report. She is with child
    And he that got it, sentenced – a young man
    More fit to do another such offence
    Than die for this.   15

The Duke questions Juliet. She declares her love for Claudio and repents of her sin. The Duke cautions her that repentance must be genuine. She is horrified to learn that Claudio will die tomorrow.

1 Juliet: what's she like? (in small groups)

This is the only time Juliet speaks in the play. Read aloud several times all she says, then compile a list of features you can deduce about her personality.

How would you account for the fact that Juliet's feelings and story have been little discussed in the millions of words written on the play?

2 Women are more to blame – or are they? (in pairs)

Presumably, the majority of people in Shakespeare's day would not find it odd that the Duke says that Juliet's 'sin' is greater than Claudio's (line 28). Juliet herself agrees with the Duke's view that her sin is 'heavier'.

Talk together about the impressions you have formed about the attitude to women in the play so far. Gather lines to justify your impressions. How have attitudes to 'shame' changed since Shakespeare's day?

3 Juliet interrupts the 'friar'

If you found lines 30–4 difficult, so have many others. One probable meaning is that true repentance is offered to Heaven, not to ease one's own feelings. With this in mind, suggest how Juliet's interruption at lines 35–6 might be spoken.

4 Stage the scene (in groups of three)

Experiment with different ways of staging this short scene. Try out different movement, gestures and tones of voice to bring out the personalities of the Duke, the Provost and Juliet.

---

arraign put on trial
'Tis meet so That's very proper
Benedicite bless you

injurious love . . . horror! my pregnancy saves me from execution, but I shall always live with the horror of Claudio's death

58

DUKE When must he die?
PROVOST   As I do think, tomorrow.
         [*To Juliet*] I have provided for you, stay awhile
         And you shall be conducted.
DUKE Repent you, fair one, of the sin you carry?
JULIET I do, and bear the shame most patiently.   20
DUKE I'll teach you how you shall arraign your conscience
         And try your penitence if it be sound
         Or hollowly put on.
JULIET   I'll gladly learn.
DUKE Love you the man that wronged you?
JULIET Yes, as I love the woman that wronged him.   25
DUKE So then it seems your most offenceful act
         Was mutually committed.
JULIET   Mutually.
DUKE Then was your sin of heavier kind than his.
JULIET I do confess it, and repent it, father.
DUKE 'Tis meet so, daughter, but lest you do repent   30
         As that the sin hath brought you to this shame –
         Which sorrow is always toward ourselves not heaven,
         Showing we would not spare heaven as we love it,
         But as we stand in fear –
JULIET I do repent me as it is an evil   35
         And take the shame with joy.
DUKE   There rest.
         Your partner, as I hear, must die tomorrow,
         And I am going with instruction to him.
         Grace go with you, *Benedicite*.   *Exit*
JULIET Must die tomorrow? Oh, injurious love   40
         That respites me a life whose very comfort
         Is still a dying horror!
PROVOST   'Tis pity of him.
                                        Exeunt

Angelo broods on his obsession for Isabella. He acknowledges his hypocrisy in not really being like his outward appearance. Human emotions will emerge; evil is evil, however it is disguised.

1 Whisper, confession or lecture? (in groups of three)

Try these five ways of speaking lines 1–17, then decide how you think Angelo should speak the lines on stage:

- whisper them to the others as a great secret
- you are on the psychoanalyst's couch, telling your thoughts
- as a public lecture
- as a prayer
- in confession, telling a priest.

2 'Blood, thou art blood' (in pairs)

Angelo argues that human emotions cannot be always hidden behind the trappings of office. Passion and desire cannot be ignored.

Talk together about whether judges can be objective. Can they avoid letting their personal feelings affect their judgements?

3 False seeming (in small groups)

Great public office can deceive fools and wise people alike, broods Angelo in lines 12–15. But he goes on to assert that an evil nature will inevitably reveal itself in spite of all respectable disguise. Even if you describe the Devil as 'Good Angel', it won't be recognised as his true description ('crest') because it is impossible to disguise his true nature.

How far do group members agree on each of the following statements?

- Evil will always reveal itself.
- There is no such thing as 'evil'.
- Society causes individuals to behave badly.

---

several separate
invention imagination
chew his name speak God's name
conception desire
state statecraft (art of government)
sere withered

boot advantage
plume feather on a helmet
place status, rank
form dignity
case, habit outward show
crest heraldic sign

ACT 2   SCENE 4
A room in Angelo's house

Enter ANGELO

ANGELO When I would pray and think, I think and pray
To several subjects: heaven hath my empty words
Whilst my invention, hearing not my tongue,
Anchors on Isabel. Heaven in my mouth
As if I did but only chew his name,   5
And in my heart the strong and swelling evil
Of my conception. The state whereon I studied
Is like a good thing being often read
Grown sere and tedious. Yea, my gravity,
Wherein – let no man hear me – I take pride,   10
Could I with boot change for an idle plume
Which the air beats for vain. Oh place, oh form,
How often dost thou with thy case, thy habit,
Wrench awe from fools and tie the wiser souls
To thy false seeming. Blood, thou art blood: 15
Let's write 'Good Angel' on the devil's horn,
'Tis not the devil's crest. How now, who's there?

Enter SERVANT

SERVANT One Isabel, a sister, desires access to you.
ANGELO Teach her the way.
                                               [*Exit Servant*]
                    Oh, heavens,
Why does my blood thus muster to my heart,   20
Making both it unable for itself
And dispossessing all my other parts
Of necessary fitness?

Angelo vehemently condemns sexual misbehaviour as equivalent to murder. Isabella is more forgiving. Angelo hints at his real intentions: her brother's life for her body.

1 'Anchors on Isabel' (in pairs)

In this second meeting, Angelo will make clear his sexual desires. Take a part each and read through from line 30 to the end of the scene. Angelo is lusting after Isabella, but it takes her some time fully to grasp his real intentions.

2 Images of Isabella

Study these two photographs of Isabella. How do different costumes create different effects (on Angelo's feelings; on your own expectations; on audience response)?

3 Measure for measure

Angelo weighs murder against sexual misdemeanours and finds them equally wrong. Work out the other comparison Angelo makes in lines 41–8 (it is an image that runs through the play – see pages 4 and 184).

---

throngs crowds
general subject the people
Quit their own part stop work, leave their proper places
fitted prepared (confessed his sins)
from nature . . . made murdered

coin forge (illegally make)
heaven's image children
stamps that are forbid illegal ways
pose question
compelled sins . . . account forced wrongs are no wrongs

So play the foolish throngs with one that swoons,
Come all to help him and so stop the air   25
By which he should revive; and even so
The general subject to a well-wished king
Quit their own part and in obsequious fondness
Crowd to his presence, where their untaught love
Must needs appear offence.

Enter ISABELLA

                        How now, fair maid?   30
ISABELLA I am come to know your pleasure.
ANGELO That you might know it would much better please me
        Than to demand what 'tis. Your brother cannot live.
ISABELLA Even so. Heaven keep your honour.
ANGELO Yet may he live a while – and it may be   35
        As long as you or I – yet he must die.
ISABELLA Under your sentence?
ANGELO   Yea.
ISABELLA When, I beseech you? That, in his reprieve,
        Longer or shorter, he may be so fitted
        That his soul sicken not.   40
ANGELO Ha! Fie, these filthy vices! It were as good
        To pardon him that hath from nature stolen
        A man already made, as to remit
        Their saucy sweetness, that do coin heaven's image
        In stamps that are forbid. 'Tis all as easy   45
        Falsely to take away a life true made
        As to put metal in restrainèd means
        To make a false one.
ISABELLA 'Tis set down so in heaven, but not in earth.
ANGELO Say you so? Then I shall pose you quickly.   50
        Which had you rather: that the most just law
        Now took your brother's life, or to redeem him
        Give up your body to such sweet uncleanness
        As she that he hath stained?
ISABELLA   Sir, believe this:
        I had rather give my body than my soul.   55
ANGELO I talk not of your soul. Our compelled sins
        Stand more for number than for accompt.
ISABELLA How say you?

Isabella, still unaware of Angelo's intentions, sees little real sin in sparing Claudio. Angelo speaks more directly: would she trade her body for Claudio's life?

1 Measure for measure (in pairs)

Angelo balances 'sin' and 'charity' in line 68. He has in mind Isabella's virginity in exchange for Claudio's life. But Isabella has a different equation in mind: Angelo's leniency in pardoning Claudio in exchange for her prayers.

Angelo and Isabella use 'sin', but each means something quite different by it. Read lines 61–73 aloud, but each time you come to 'sin' (or 'it'), say what each character has in mind.

2 Do black masks enhance beauty?

Angelo suspects that wisdom or beauty is more attractive when it is concealed (lines 78–81). But the expression 'black masks' is puzzling. It might mean the black veil worn by nuns; or the masks that women in the audience wear; or masks worn to protect against the sun.

Suggest what Angelo might do, as he speaks the lines, to make his meaning clear.

3 Just suppose . . . (in pairs)

In lines 87–98 Angelo puts a hypothetical case to Isabella (just suppose you were fancied by an important person with the power to spare Claudio . . .). But he clearly has something else in mind. Try these two ways of speaking the lines:

- Say them in the most shifty, untrustworthy manner you can.
- Substitute actual names for the indirect words Angelo uses (for example, Claudio, Isabella or Angelo for 'his', 'you', 'such a person', and so on).

How do you think Angelo should speak the lines?

---

warrant that say that's true
a peril to my soul my own sin
charity loving mercy
suit plea
your answer your responsibility
tax criticise, accuse
enshield concealed

Accountant Accountable
As I . . . question But I'm only supposing
fetch release
treasures of your body your virginity
this supposed this person

ANGELO Nay, I'll not warrant that, for I can speak
                Against the thing I say. Answer to this: 60
                I, now the voice of the recorded law,
                Pronounce a sentence on your brother's life.
                Might there not be a charity in sin
                To save this brother's life?
ISABELLA   Please you to do't,
                I'll take it as a peril to my soul,   65
                It is no sin at all but charity.
ANGELO Pleased you to do't, at peril of your soul,
                Were equal poise of sin and charity.
ISABELLA That I do beg his life, if it be sin,
                Heaven let me bear it. You granting of my suit,   70
                If that be sin, I'll make it my morn-prayer
                To have it added to the faults of mine
                And nothing of your answer.
ANGELO   Nay, but hear me,
                Your sense pursues not mine: either you are ignorant
                Or seem so crafty, and that's not good.   75
ISABELLA Let me be ignorant and in nothing good
                But graciously to know I am no better.
ANGELO Thus wisdom wishes to appear most bright
                When it doth tax itself, as these black masks
                Proclaim an enshield beauty ten times louder   80
                Than beauty could, displayed. But mark me.
                To be received plain, I'll speak more gross:
                Your brother is to die.
ISABELLA So.
ANGELO And his offence is so as it appears   85
                Accountant to the law upon that pain.
ISABELLA True.
ANGELO Admit no other way to save his life –
                As I subscribe not that, nor any other,
                But in the loss of question – that you, his sister,   90
                Finding yourself desired of such a person
                Whose credit with the judge, or own great place,
                Could fetch your brother from the manacles
                Of the all-binding law, and that there were
                No earthly mean to save him, but that either   95
                You must lay down the treasures of your body
                To this supposed, or else to let him suffer:
                What would you do?

Isabella says that she prefers death to shame and everlasting damnation.
Angelo reminds her of her earlier light dismissal of Claudio's crime. When
Isabella describes women's frailty, Angelo pounces.

---

1 An erotic image? (in pairs)

Isabella's lines 100–4 are filled with sexually ambivalent language: 'keen whips', 'rubies', 'strip', 'bed', 'longing'. But in lines 106–9 her language is wholly religious (better Claudio should die than she suffer eternal damnation caused by sexual misbehaviour).

Talk together about whether you agree with one student's view that 'these lines show her as masochistic, sexually frustrated and religiously confused'.

'St Teresa of Avila' by Bernini.
Many people think this sculpture of
religious ecstasy also depicts sexual
experience. Does it echo Isabella's
lines 100–4?

2 Angelo's intentions (in small groups)

Angelo has made three attempts to put the 'virginity exchanged for life' bargain to Isabella. She clearly rejects it, and seems not to know that it is Angelo himself who desires her. Angelo is trying all kinds of ways to test her, to make her receptive to his proposal.

One person reads aloud each remark Angelo makes opposite. The others comment after each remark on how they think it should be said, and on Angelo's intention in making it.

---

cheaper way preferable action
die for ever be damned eternally
ignomy shame, ignominy
of two houses two different things
nothing kin no relation
of late in our previous conversation
fedary accomplice

owe and succeed own and inherit
(the sense of 122–4 is 'let Claudio
die if no other men are similarly
weak')
forms reflections
credulous to false prints easily
deceived (believe forgeries)

ISABELLA As much for my poor brother as myself:
      That is, were I under the terms of death,   100
      Th'impression of keen whips I'd wear as rubies,
      And strip myself to death as to a bed
      That longing have been sick for, ere I'd yield
      My body up to shame.
ANGELO Then must your brother die.   105
ISABELLA And 'twere the cheaper way:
      Better it were a brother died at once,
      Than that a sister by redeeming him
      Should die for ever.
ANGELO Were not you then as cruel as the sentence   110
      That you have slandered so?
ISABELLA Ignomy in ransom and free pardon
      Are of two houses: lawful mercy
      Is nothing kin to foul redemption.
ANGELO You seemed of late to make the law a tyrant,   115
      And rather proved the sliding of your brother
      A merriment than a vice.
ISABELLA Oh, pardon me my lord, it oft falls out
      To have what we would have, we speak not what we mean.
      I something do excuse the thing I hate   120
      For his advantage that I dearly love.
ANGELO We are all frail.
ISABELLA   Else let my brother die,
      If not a fedary but only he
      Owe and succeed thy weakness.
ANGELO Nay, women are frail too.   125
ISABELLA Ay, as the glasses where they view themselves,
      Which are as easy broke as they make forms.
      Women? Help heaven, men their creation mar
      In profiting by them. Nay, call us ten times frail,
      For we are soft as our complexions are,   130
      And credulous to false prints.
ANGELO   I think it well,
      And from this testimony of your own sex –
      Since I suppose we are made to be no stronger
      Than faults may shake our frames – let me be bold;

Angelo declares his 'love'. Isabella threatens to denounce him. Angelo says that she will not be believed, and makes utterly clear his bargain: sexual intercourse in exchange for Claudio's life.

1 Taunting Isabella (in groups of six to eight)

Explore the dramatic effect of lines 155–71 in different ways. One person is Isabella, surrounded by the others, who share the lines, speaking only to a punctuation mark, then handing over to the next person.

- sneer them
- whisper them
- shout them

- speak them mockingly
- speak them angrily
- speak them menacingly

- say each section twice
- accompany with gestures
- speak them haughtily

Take decisions about how you think Angelo should deliver them on stage.

2 Actions!

Look back over the whole exchange between Angelo and Isabella in this scene. Write notes, with appropriate line references, to help the two actors with movement, gesture and facial expressions (for example, does Angelo touch Isabella? At what point does Isabella really understand Angelo's true intention? What does she do to show it? What moods does she show at lines 141, 153–5?). Your notes should show how your staging can heighten the drama.

---

arrest take you at
external warrants appearances
the destined livery what nature
  intends
I know . . . others you speak falsely
  in order to test me

seeming hypocrisy
proclaim expose, denounce
vouch word
calumny false accusation
prolixious over-abundant

I do arrest your words. Be that you are,   135
That is, a woman; if you be more, you're none.
If you be one, as you are well expressed
By all external warrants, show it now
By putting on the destined livery.
ISABELLA I have no tongue but one. Gentle my lord,   140
Let me entreat you speak the former language.
ANGELO Plainly conceive, I love you.
ISABELLA My brother did love Juliet
And you tell me that he shall die for't.
ANGELO He shall not, Isabel, if you give me love.   145
ISABELLA I know your virtue hath a licence in't
Which seems a little fouler than it is
To pluck on others.
ANGELO   Believe me on mine honour,
My words express my purpose.
ISABELLA Ha! Little honour to be much believed,   150
And most pernicious purpose. Seeming, seeming.
I will proclaim thee, Angelo, look for't.
Sign me a present pardon for my brother,
Or with an outstretched throat I'll tell the world aloud
What man thou art.
ANGELO   Who will believe thee, Isabel?   155
My unsoiled name, th'austereness of my life,
My vouch against you, and my place i'th'state,
Will so your accusation overweigh
That you shall stifle in your own report
And smell of calumny. I have begun,   160
And now I give my sensual race the rein.
Fit thy consent to my sharp appetite,
Lay by all nicety and prolixious blushes
That banish what they sue for, redeem thy brother
By yielding up thy body to my will,   165
Or else he must not only die the death
But thy unkindness shall his death draw out
To lingering sufferance. Answer me tomorrow,
Or by th'affection that now guides me most
I'll prove a tyrant to him. As for you,   170
Say what you can, my false o'erweighs your true.   *Exit*

69

Isabella realises that no one will believe her story. Angelo has the power to bend the law to serve his desires. She resolves to visit Claudio. Rather than yield up her chastity, she must let him die.

1 'More than our brother is our chastity' (in small groups)

- Talk together about what line 186 tells you about Isabella.
- The actress playing Isabella says to you, 'It just doesn't seem possible to me. Of course she should give in to Angelo to save Claudio. So how can I possibly say it? I'll need a great deal of convincing and help.' Convince her and help her.
- 'This is the most embarrassing line in the play. Modern audiences simply cannot believe it.' What would you reply to the student who made this remark?

2 Isabella's soliloquy

Alone on stage, Isabella agonisingly considers her predicament. Does she speak direct to the audience? To herself? To an image or prop?

Work out Isabella's tone, movements and gestures for each sentence.

3 Measure for measure

Isabella repeatedly weighs one thing against another. Read her lines aloud. Use your hands to show each time she weighs or balances one thing against another. Then make a list of each thing or person she 'balances' against another. Which 'outweigh' which?

4 Make a conversation (in pairs)

At the end of this scene, both Angelo and Isabella have seventeen lines each. Each speech has six sentences. Construct a conversation or dialogue from the twelve sentences. You can re-order them and 'inter-cut' them to make the most dramatically effective presentation.

---

approof approval
Bidding . . . draws making the law servant to their lust

prompture prompting, urging
bloody blocks execution blocks

ISABELLA To whom should I complain? Did I tell this
        Who would believe me? Oh, perilous mouths
        That bear in them one and the self-same tongue,
        Either of condemnation or approof,   175
        Bidding the law make curtsey to their will,
        Hooking both right and wrong to th'appetite
        To follow as it draws. I'll to my brother.
        Though he hath fall'n by prompture of the blood
        Yet hath he in him such a mind of honour   180
        That had he twenty heads to tender down
        On twenty bloody blocks he'd yield them up
        Before his sister should her body stoop
        To such abhorred pollution.
        Then Isabel live chaste, and brother die: 185
        More than our brother is our chastity.
        I'll tell him yet of Angelo's request,
        And fit his mind to death for his soul's rest.   *Exit*

Looking back at Act 2
Activities for groups or individuals

1 Changing emotions

Find a way to map the progress of the dramatic swings in Angelo's emotions in Scenes 2 and 4. If you draw a chart or graph, identify each line in the script where Angelo's mood changes.

Make a similar graph or chart of Isabella's changing feelings throughout these two scenes. Compare your two diagrams.

2 On the frontier

You are a group of refugees fleeing from a merciless invading army. They will kill you if they catch you. At the border post, the Captain of the Guard refuses to let you pass unless one young woman in the group has sexual intercourse with him. He gives you fifteen minutes to decide. . . . Improvise what happens in those fifteen minutes.

3 Echoes and parallels

The comic sub-plot provides an ironic commentary on the themes of sexuality, justice and deceit. It reflects the confusion about morality, legality and identity in Vienna as it reveals:

- the corruption that has resulted from the Duke's lax rule
- Mistress Elbow, like Juliet, is 'with child'
- a distorted mirror-image of the justice meted out to Claudio
- how difficult it is to reach the truth in any legal dispute (as Pompey's absurd and convoluted story shows)
- Elbow calls Angelo a 'varlet' (he will prove to be just that)
- Angelo leaves Escalus to clear up the mess (the Duke similarly abdicated)
- Angelo's latent sadism ('whip them all').

Select one or more of these parallels. Find ways of illustrating them vividly (for example, physically, or as a drawing, or in writing).

4 The sticking place?

Is there a point beyond which you would not go to save the life of a loved relative or friend? What is it? What might a brother refuse to do to save his sister's life?

5 Bad laws?

In Scene 1 Pompey is sceptical that the law against fornication can be enforced. It goes against human nature. In the 1920s the government of the USA attempted to enforce Prohibition: the banning of alcohol. The result was widespread criminal activity as 'bootleggers' (illegal liquor traders) flouted the law to make alcohol widely available.

Organise a class debate on the motion 'Laws that go against human nature can never succeed'.

6 A man's world

'The trouble with Vienna', wrote one student, 'is that it's a man's world. Men make, enforce, judge and corrupt the law.' List examples that support or challenge her claim. Do you agree with her?

7 Does Good provoke Evil?

Isabella's virtue provokes Angelo's desire to destroy it ('Dost thou desire her foully for those things/That make her good?'). Does the sight of goodness provoke some people to destroy that very goodness? Use actual examples from today's world as a basis for your discussion.

8 Symbols of authority

Mercy, says Isabella, is more fitting to people holding great authority than crowns, swords, staffs of office, or ceremonial robes (2.2.61–2). Use these symbols of authority to design the cover of a theatre programme for a production of *Measure for Measure*.

9 Only obeying orders?

Angelo argues (2.4.55–6) that an evil you are forced to commit ('compelled sins') isn't really an evil. His words sound rather like the excuse 'I was only obeying orders'. Talk together about whether you agree that crimes you are forced to commit are not really crimes at all. Begin by taking the case of a soldier accused of war crimes.

10 'What I want most is . . .'

For each character in Act 2, write a sentence which begins 'What I want most is . . .'. Compare your sentences with another student's.

The Duke urges Claudio to adopt a stoical acceptance of death. He asserts that life is a miserable condition, subject to many afflictions and fears.

1 The Duke's speech on death

The Duke offers Claudio a classic set of theological consolations for death. In Christian doctrine of the time, humankind is at once a mortal and an immortal being, commanded to live and breed upon the earth whilst simultaneously preparing for death and promised afterlife in Heaven. The 'friar'-Duke's list of life's vanities is reminiscent of the *Ars Moriendi* ('The Art of Dying'), a text which would have been commonly known in sixteenth-century England. Yet the Duke's deeply pessimistic version lacks a real spiritual dimension; nobility, valour, happiness were meant to be God-given gifts. Choose one of the following to explore lines 5–41:

a Create the atmosphere (in small groups)
Experiment with ways of presenting the speech. Share out the lines. Add music (Fauré's *Requiem* makes an evocative background). Try whispering the lines, or saying them sadly, cynically or vehemently. Make your own presentation atmospherically dramatic.

b Answer back! (in pairs)
Divide the Duke's speech into separate arguments – the second person to interrupt and argue the opposite case. Show your 'dialogue' to the rest of the class.

c Further reading
In Sonnet 146 Shakespeare describes death as a consolation to a troubled soul. Find a copy of Shakespeare's *Sonnets* in your school or college library and compare the words of Sonnet 146 with the Duke's speech here. What similarities do you discover?

---

absolute resolved
Servile . . . influences subject to the stars' influence
keepst dwell
accommodations advantages, endowments

fork of a poor worm tongue of a miserable snake
no more no worse than sleep
complexion mood, behaviour
after the moon affected by the waxing and waning of the moon
ingots gold bars

Enter DUKE disguised as a friar, CLAUDIO and PROVOST

DUKE So then you hope of pardon from Lord Angelo?
CLAUDIO The miserable have no other medicine
      But only hope.
      I have hope to live, and am prepared to die.
DUKE Be absolute for death: either death or life   5
      Shall thereby be the sweeter. Reason thus with life:
      If I do lose thee I do lose a thing
      That none but fools would keep; a breath thou art,
      Servile to all the skyey influences
      That dost this habitation where thou keepst   10
      Hourly afflict. Merely, thou art death's fool,
      For him thou labour'st by thy flight to shun
      And yet runn'st toward him still. Thou art not noble,
      For all th'accommodations that thou bear'st
      Are nursed by baseness; thou'rt by no means valiant,   15
      For thou dost fear the soft and tender fork
      Of a poor worm. Thy best of rest is sleep,
      And that thou oft provok'st, yet grossly fear'st
      Thy death, which is no more. Thou art not thyself,
      For thou exists on many a thousand grains   20
      That issue out of dust. Happy thou art not,
      For what thou hast not still thou striv'st to get,
      And what thou hast, forget'st. Thou art not certain,
      For thy complexion shifts to strange effects
      After the moon. If thou art rich thou'rt poor,   25
      For like an ass whose back with ingots bows
      Thou bear'st thy heavy riches but a journey
      And death unloads thee. Friend hast thou none,

Claudio thanks the 'friar' for his advice, and says he is ready for death. The Duke and the Provost hide in order to eavesdrop on Claudio and Isabella. She tells her brother to prepare for death.

1 Stage direction (in groups of four)

At line 52 the Duke and the Provost 'conceal themselves' to overhear the private conversation between brother and sister. Discuss how you would enact the stage direction if you were directing the play. Would the two hidden characters remain visible to the audience? Could they go right off-stage? Act out lines 40–62, experimenting with different presentations.

2 'Comfort' and 'remedy' (in pairs or groups of three)

Both Claudio and Isabella use the words 'comfort' (lines 53 and 55) and 'remedy' (lines 60 and 61). Talk together about what you think each character means by the words, and how significant any difference in definition might be. Explore ways of presenting the words and the tensions in different usages. Show your presentation to the rest of the class.

3 Physical images

Isabella says that 'to save a head' would be to 'cleave a heart in twain'. What do you think she means by this? Create a design on paper depicting these two physical images.

---

bowels children
proper loins own body
serpigo skin disease
rheum mucus
palsied eld trembling old age

moe more
sue to live plead for life
lieger consul, ambassador
appointment preparations

For thine own bowels which do call thee sire,
The mere effusion of thy proper loins,   30
Do curse the gout, serpigo, and the rheum
For ending thee no sooner. Thou hast nor youth nor age,
But as it were an after-dinner's sleep,
Dreaming on both: for all thy blessèd youth
Becomes as agèd and doth beg the alms   35
Of palsied eld; and when thou art old and rich,
Thou hast neither heat, affection, limb, nor beauty
To make thy riches pleasant. What's yet in this
That bears the name of life? Yet in this life
Lie hid moe thousand deaths; yet death we fear   40
That makes these odds all even.
CLAUDIO   I humbly thank you.
    To sue to live, I find I seek to die,
    And seeking death, find life: let it come on.
ISABELLA [Within] What ho, peace here; grace and good company.
PROVOST Who's there? Come in, the wish deserves a welcome. 45
DUKE [To Claudio] Dear sir, ere long I'll visit you again.
CLAUDIO Most holy sir, I thank you.

                    Enter ISABELLA

ISABELLA My business is a word or two with Claudio.
PROVOST And very welcome. Look, signior, here's your sister.
DUKE Provost, a word with you.   50
PROVOST As many as you please.
DUKE Bring me to hear them speak where I may be concealed.
                    [*Duke and Provost conceal themselves*]
CLAUDIO Now, sister, what's the comfort?
ISABELLA Why,
    As all comforts are: most good, most good indeed.   55
    Lord Angelo, having affairs to heaven,
    Intends you for his swift ambassador,
    Where you shall be an everlasting lieger;
    Therefore your best appointment make with speed,
    Tomorrow you set on.
CLAUDIO   Is there no remedy?   60
ISABELLA None, but such remedy as, to save a head,
    To cleave a heart in twain.
CLAUDIO   But is there any?

> *Isabella says there is an alternative to Claudio's execution, but it is dishonourable and shameful. Claudio claims that he will face death without fear. Isabella reveals Angelo's proposition.*

1 Act it out (in pairs)

Read the whole scene between brother and sister through (lines 53–150). Experiment with different ways of speaking and explore the possible ways of presenting the relationship between Isabella and Claudio. Is there any point at which you think that Isabella feels confident that her brother will respond sympathetically to her dilemma?

2 Embracing death (in small groups)

Claudio says that he will 'encounter darkness as a bride . . .' (lines 83–4). Create a group tableau based on this image which combines both love (sex) and death. How appropriate an image is it for Claudio to use – particularly at this point in the play?

3 Freeze the moment (in groups of four)

Take Isabella's lines:

'If I would yield him my virginity
Thou might'st be freed!' (lines 97–8)

and freeze the moment as if on stage. Choose a character each (Isabella, Claudio, Duke, Provost) and role-play what you think the thoughts of each would be at this precise moment. Present your ideas to the rest of the class.

4 'The sense of death is most in apprehension' (in small groups)

Talk together about how much you agree or disagree with Isabella's claim that fearing death is worse than death itself.

---

perpetual durance everlasting imprisonment
vastidity expanse, vastness
determined scope fixed limit
bark strip (like bark from a tree)
corporal sufferance physical pain

a resolution fetch gain courage
appliances tricks, devices
settled visage grave face
enew drive into the water (and kill)
cast scoured, cleansed
prenzie precious *or* precise

ISABELLA Yes, brother, you may live;
    There is a devilish mercy in the judge,
    If you'll implore it, that will free your life,   65
    But fetter you till death.
CLAUDIO   Perpetual durance?
ISABELLA Ay, just, perpetual durance, a restraint,
    Though all the world's vastidity you had,
    To a determined scope.
CLAUDIO   But in what nature?
ISABELLA In such a one as you, consenting to't,   70
    Would bark your honour from that trunk you bear
    And leave you naked.
CLAUDIO   Let me know the point.
ISABELLA Oh, I do fear thee, Claudio, and I quake
    Lest thou a feverous life shouldst entertain
    And six or seven winters more respect   75
    Than a perpetual honour. Dar'st thou die?
    The sense of death is most in apprehension,
    And the poor beetle that we tread upon
    In corporal sufferance finds a pang as great
    As when a giant dies.
CLAUDIO   Why give you me this shame?   80
    Think you I can a resolution fetch
    From flowery tenderness? If I must die
    I will encounter darkness as a bride
    And hug it in mine arms.
ISABELLA There spake my brother, there my father's grave   85
    Did utter forth a voice. Yes, thou must die:
    Thou art too noble to conserve a life
    In base appliances. This outward-sainted deputy
    Whose settled visage and deliberate word
    Nips youth i'th'head and follies doth enew   90
    As falcon doth the fowl, is yet a devil:
    His filth within being cast, he would appear
    A pond as deep as hell.
CLAUDIO   The prenzie Angelo?
ISABELLA Oh 'tis the cunning livery of hell
    The damned'st body to invest and cover   95
    In prenzie guards. Dost thou think, Claudio,
    If I would yield him my virginity
    Thou might'st be freed!

Claudio is initially shocked by Angelo's proposition, but then begins to see it as a way of escaping execution. He graphically describes his very real fear of death.

1 Claudio's changing feelings (in pairs)

Collect together Claudio's responses to Isabella's words (at lines 98, 102, 105, 109–10, 116) and trace the progression through them of his thoughts and feelings. Present these lines as a series of 'snapshots'.

2 Two concepts of death (in groups of about ten)

Read through the Duke's homily to Claudio on dying (lines 5–41). Then read through Claudio's graphic description of his vision of death (lines 118–32). Split your group into two, one half taking the Duke's speech, the other working with Claudio's. Each sub-group needs to divide the speech up between them, either learning sections or jotting down each individual's lines on card. You will need to discuss in detail exactly how to divide the speech into sections.

When you have familiarised yourself with the lines, bring both sub-groups together again. First of all, simply take it in turn to speak alternately, inter-cutting one speech with the other. Discuss what new resonances you now notice about the two speeches, then work on ways of presenting them dramatically to the rest of the class. Experiment with movement, sound and lighting if you can get use of a drama studio for the lesson.

---

rank corrupt
force enforce
perdurably fined punished for eternity
cold obstruction rigor mortis

thrilling piercing
viewless invisible
pendent suspended
lawless and incertain uncontrolled and uncertain

CLAUDIO   Oh, heavens, it cannot be!
ISABELLA Yes, he would give't thee; from this rank offence
    So to offend him still. This night's the time   100
    That I should do what I abhor to name,
    Or else thou diest tomorrow.
CLAUDIO   Thou shalt not do't.
ISABELLA Oh, were it but my life
    I'd throw it down for your deliverance
    As frankly as a pin.
CLAUDIO   Thanks, dear Isabel.   105
ISABELLA Be ready, Claudio, for your death tomorrow.
CLAUDIO Yes. Has he affections in him,
    That thus can make him bite the law by th'nose
    When he would force it? Sure it is no sin,
    Or of the deadly seven it is the least.   110
ISABELLA Which is the least?
CLAUDIO If it were damnable, he, being so wise,
    Why would he for the momentary trick
    Be perdurably fined? Oh Isabel!
ISABELLA What says my brother?   115
CLAUDIO Death is a fearful thing.
ISABELLA And shamèd life a hateful.
CLAUDIO Ay, but to die and go we know not where,
    To lie in cold obstruction and to rot,
    This sensible warm motion to become   120
    A kneaded clod, and the delighted spirit
    To bathe in fiery floods or to reside
    In thrilling region of thick-ribbed ice,
    To be imprisoned in the viewless winds
    And blown with restless violence round about   125
    The pendent world, or to be worse than worst
    Of those that lawless and incertain thought
    Imagine howling; 'tis too horrible.
    The weariest and most loathèd worldly life
    That age, ache, penury, and imprisonment   130
    Can lay on nature, is a paradise
    To what we fear of death.
ISABELLA   Alas, alas.

Claudio pleads with Isabella to give in to Angelo and so save his life. She turns on him angrily. The Duke tells Claudio that Angelo is only testing Isabella's virtue, not intending to molest her.

1 'Sweet sister, let me live' (in groups of ten to fifteen)

Stand in a large circle. Divide Isabella's words to her brother (lines 136–51) between all group members. Memorise your own piece of script, then place one group member in the centre of the circle. S/he has the line 'Sweet sister, let me live', and can implore any members of the circle with those words. Those in the circle reply using their learnt phrase or line, speaking it in any way they feel appropriate.

2 Claudio's argument (in pairs)

Claudio argues that any act Isabella undertakes in order to save her brother's life can't be a sin – and indeed becomes a positive virtue! Read through Claudio's words (lines 133–6) and say what you think of his argument.

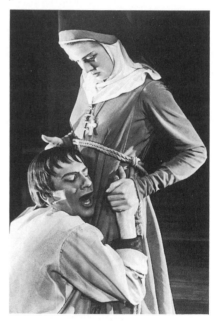

3 Production photo

Can you identify the line being spoken?

Heaven . . . fair God forbid that my mother deceived my father
warpèd slip of wilderness perverted bastard (or unnatural child)
bending down praying

Mercy . . . bawd Pardoning you would lead to further sexual offences
an assay a test
confessor priest who hears confession

CLAUDIO Sweet sister, let me live.
What sin you do to save a brother's life,
Nature dispenses with the deed so far   135
That it becomes a virtue.
ISABELLA   Oh, you beast!
Oh faithless coward, oh dishonest wretch!
Wilt thou be made a man out of my vice?
Is't not a kind of incest to take life
From thine own sister's shame? What should I think?   140
Heaven shield my mother played my father fair,
For such a warpèd slip of wilderness
Ne'er issued from his blood. Take my defiance,
Die, perish. Might but my bending down
Reprieve thee from thy fate, it should proceed.   145
I'll pray a thousand prayers for thy death,
No word to save thee.
CLAUDIO Nay hear me, Isabel.
ISABELLA   Oh, fie, fie, fie!
Thy sin's not accidental, but a trade.
Mercy to thee would prove itself a bawd,   150
'Tis best that thou diest quickly.
CLAUDIO   Oh hear me, Isabella.
DUKE [*Coming from concealment*]
Vouchsafe a word, young sister, but one word.
ISABELLA What is your will?
DUKE Might you dispense with your leisure, I would by and by have
some speech with you: the satisfaction I would require is likewise   155
your own benefit.
ISABELLA I have no superfluous leisure, my stay must be stolen out
of other affairs – but I will attend you a while.
DUKE [*To Claudio*] Son, I have overheard what hath passed between
you and your sister. Angelo had never the purpose to corrupt   160
her; only he hath made an assay of her virtue, to practise his
judgement with the disposition of natures. She, having the truth
of honour in her, hath made him that gracious denial which he is
most glad to receive. I am confessor to Angelo and I know this to
be true, therefore prepare yourself to death. Do not satisfy your   165
resolution with hopes that are fallible, tomorrow you must die:
go to your knees and make ready.

83

Left alone with Isabella, the Duke tells her that he has a plan involving a woman called Mariana. It will not only save Claudio but also enable Isabella to retain her virginity.

---

1 Brother and sister: last words

The last words which Isabella and Claudio exchange in the play are those at lines 151 and 152, when Isabella tells her brother: ''Tis best that thou diest quickly'. But in the 1987 Royal Shakespeare Company production, Claudio spoke line 168 directly to his sister rather than to the Duke. What difference would that make? If you were directing the play, what would you do at line 168, and why?

2 Friar and nun (in pairs)

Read the Duke's words to Isabella 'The hand . . . ever fair' (lines 176–9). Imagine different contexts for the lines, for example:

- a father and a daughter speaking
- a ruler and a subject
- a father and a son
- two lovers
- a friar and a nun.

Act out each context above with your partner, and discuss what difference in style each version demands. Talk about how you think the words should be said by the Duke in your own production of the play, and what this implies about the relationship between the two characters.

3 'Virtue is bold, and goodness never fearful'

Line 199 could be the motto for a coat of arms for Isabella. Design a heraldic shield for her, using the line.

---

sue plead	**resolve** inform
habit friar's robes	**discover** expose
complexion nature	**avoid** deny
hath examples gives precedents	**peradventure** perhaps
content this substitute satisfy Angelo	**miscarried** was shipwrecked

CLAUDIO Let me ask my sister pardon. I am so out of love with life
that I will sue to be rid of it.

DUKE Hold you there. Farewell. Provost, a word with you.   170

PROVOST [*Coming from concealment*] What's your will, father?

DUKE That now you are come, you will be gone: leave me a while
with the maid; my mind promises, with my habit, no loss shall
touch her by my company.

PROVOST In good time.   175

Exit Provost [and Claudio]

DUKE [*To Isabella*] The hand that hath made you fair hath made you
good: the goodness that is cheap in beauty makes beauty brief in
goodness; but grace, being the soul of your complexion, shall
keep the body of it ever fair. The assault that Angelo hath made
to you, fortune hath conveyed to my understanding, and but that   180
frailty hath examples for his falling, I should wonder at Angelo.
How will you do to content this substitute and to save your
brother?

ISABELLA I am now going to resolve him. I had rather my brother die
by the law than my son should be unlawfully born; but oh, how   185
much is the good Duke deceived in Angelo! If ever he return and
I can speak to him, I will open my lips in vain or discover his
government.

DUKE That shall not be much amiss, yet as the matter now stands he
will avoid your accusation: he made trial of you only. Therefore   190
fasten your ear on my advisings, to the love I have in doing good.
A remedy presents itself. I do make myself believe that you may
most uprighteously do a poor wronged lady a merited benefit,
redeem your brother from the angry law, do no stain to your own
gracious person, and much please the absent Duke, if peradven-   195
ture he shall ever return to have hearing of this business.

ISABELLA Let me hear you speak farther; I have spirit to do any
thing that appears not foul in the truth of my spirit.

DUKE Virtue is bold, and goodness never fearful. Have you not heard
speak of Mariana, the sister of Frederick the great soldier who   200
miscarried at sea?

ISABELLA I have heard of the lady, and good words went with her
name.

The Duke tells how Angelo jilted Mariana when she lost her dowry through her brother's death. Nevertheless, she still loves him. The Duke plans to substitute Mariana for Isabella in Angelo's illicitly proposed rendezvous.

1 Mariana is rejected (in pairs)

Improvise the incident in Mariana's life when Angelo told her that he was breaking off the engagement – and why.

2 'What think you of it?'

What do *you* think of the Duke's plan? Consider the following statements in turn and say which you agree with most strongly. Try to explain your reasons in detail:

- the plan is ingenious
- it suits everybody perfectly
- it will lead to a happy ending
- it will lead to a tragic ending
- the plan is based on lies and deceit
- the Duke is immoral and exploitative
- Isabella can never agree to it
- Mariana is being used
- the Duke is kind and merciful
- none of these, but a statement of your own.

3 Show the action (in groups of four)

Read through the Duke's proposed plan (lines 229–39) and make a list of all the 'action' which he describes. In your group find a way (for example, through mime, tableaux or improvisation) of presenting the plan to the rest of the class.

---

limit of the solemnity date fixed for the wedding
portion and sinew the whole lot
combinate betrothed
pretending . . . dishonour falsely alleging dishonourable things about her

a marble to unmoved by
refer yourself to this advantage on this condition
encounter sexual encounter
scaled weighed, judged
frame prepare, make ready

DUKE She should this Angelo have married – was affianced to her
     oath, and the nuptial appointed; between which time of the   205
     contract, and limit of the solemnity, her brother Frederick was
     wrecked at sea, having in that perished vessel the dowry of his
     sister. But mark how heavily this befell to the poor gentlewoman:
     there she lost a noble and renowned brother, in his love toward
     her ever most kind and natural; with him the portion and sinew   210
     of her fortune, her marriage dowry; with both, her combinate
     husband, this well-seeming Angelo.
ISABELLA Can this be so? Did Angelo so leave her?
DUKE Left her in her tears, and dried not one of them with his com-
     fort; swallowed his vows whole, pretending in her discoveries of 215
     dishonour: in few, bestowed her on her own lamentation, which
     she yet wears for his sake; and he, a marble to her tears, is
     washed with them, but relents not.
ISABELLA What a merit were it in death to take this poor maid from
     the world! What corruption in this life, that it will let this man 220
     live? But how out of this can she avail?
DUKE It is a rupture that you may easily heal, and the cure of it not
     only saves your brother but keeps you from dishonour in doing
     it.
ISABELLA Show me how, good father.   225
DUKE This fore-named maid hath yet in her the continuance of her
     first affection. His unjust unkindness, that in all reason should
     have quenched her love, hath like an impediment in the current
     made it more violent and unruly. Go you to Angelo, answer his
     requiring with a plausible obedience, agree with his demands to   230
     the point, only refer yourself to this advantage: first, that your
     stay with him may not be long; that the time may have all shadow
     and silence in it; and the place answer to convenience. This
     being granted in course, and now follows all: we shall advise this
     wronged maid to stead up your appointment, go in your place. If   235
     the encounter acknowledge itself hereafter, it may compel him to
     her recompense; and here, by this, is your brother saved, your
     honour untainted, the poor Mariana advantaged, and the corrupt
     deputy scaled. The maid will I frame and make fit for his
     attempt; if you think well to carry this, as you may, the double- 240
     ness of the benefit defends the deceit from reproof. What think
     you of it?

87

Isabella agrees to the Duke's plan, and leaves to set up the rendezvous with Angelo. Scene 2 opens with Elbow bringing in Pompey. The Duke asks what crime Pompey has committed.

1 Two scenes Shakespeare didn't write (in pairs)

The Duke says that he is about to go to the 'moated grange' where Mariana lives in order to explain his plan to her. Isabella is going to see Angelo to tell him that she agrees to his proposition. Choose one of these two scenes and improvise it with your partner. In each case, think about the full implication of the scene – for example, a 'friar' proposing that a woman has pre-marital sex with a man who has condemned others to death for just the same 'crime' . . .

2 Scene change? (in groups of four)

In the earliest printed copy of the play there is a break between Scene 1 and Scene 2, yet both scenes appear to take place in the prison. Consider what you would do if you were directing the play. Here are some choices:

- have no change of scene at all
- mark a complete break in the flow of action by setting it in a fresh cell
- have a split stage so that on Isabella's exit the Duke just walks over to Elbow and Pompey
- the Duke leaves the stage completely, then re-enters
- the Duke stays on stage, Elbow and Pompey enter as Isabella leaves
- the lights to go down slightly as if to mark a short passage of time.

Add your own ideas. Try acting them out in your group and decide which works best. What effect does each variation have on the 'mood' of the new scene?

---

holding up supporting role
presently immediately
moated grange secluded country house
bastard sweet Spanish wine
two usuries money-lending and prostitution

stands for the facing signals such deceit (Pompey says that prostitution is punished, but money-lending is rewarded richly, even though it is deceitful)
picklock skeleton key

ISABELLA The image of it gives me content already, and I trust it will
grow to a most prosperous perfection.

DUKE It lies much in your holding up. Haste you speedily to Angelo.   245
If for this night he entreat you to his bed, give him promise of
satisfaction. I will presently to Saint Luke's; there at the moated
grange resides this dejected Mariana; at that place call upon me,
and dispatch with Angelo, that it may be quickly.

ISABELLA I thank you for this comfort. Fare you well, good father.   250

Exit

ACT 3   SCENE 2
Vienna   The prison a few minutes later

Enter ELBOW, POMPEY, *and* OFFICERS

ELBOW Nay, if there be no remedy for it, but that you will needs buy
and sell men and women like beasts, we shall have all the world
drink brown and white bastard.

DUKE Oh heavens, what stuff is here.

POMPEY 'Twas never merry world since, of two usuries, the merriest   5
was put down and the worser allowed by order of law – a furred
gown to keep him warm, and furred with fox and lamb-skins too,
to signify that craft, being richer than innocency, stands for the
facing.

ELBOW Come your way, sir – bless you, good father friar.   10

DUKE And you, good brother father. What offence hath this man
made you, sir?

ELBOW Marry, sir, he hath offended the law; and, sir, we take him to
be a thief, too, sir, for we have found upon him, sir, a strange
pick-lock, which we have sent to the deputy.   15

The Duke condemns Pompey for living off prostitution. Elbow predicts Pompey's execution. Lucio greets Pompey, but shows no sympathy for him or for Mistress Overdone.

1 'A bawd, a wicked bawd!'

Read through the Duke's castigation of pimping (lines 16–25). Why do you think the Duke is so revolted by Pompey? How might Pompey answer the Duke's accusations if he knew what the Duke has just been planning with Isabella in the previous scene?

2 Prostitution: a filthy vice? (in groups of about five)

Imagine that a documentary programme on the subject of prostitution is being made for Vienna Television. In the studio to put forward their points of view are representatives from all sections of Viennese society: the Duke, Pompey, Mistress Overdone and Lucio. With one group member chairing the discussion, improvise the television programme, making sure you think carefully about the range of views that might be expressed by those characters.

3 History and myth

Lucio mocks Pompey, joking on his name (Julius Caesar captured the sons of Pompey the Great, and led them in triumph behind his chariot). Lucio also uses classical mythology to taunt Pompey: Pygmalion was a sculptor whose statues came to life (but 'newly made woman' might also mean prostitute here).

maw mouth	**sad and few words** in an affected
array dress	state of melancholy
Go mend go and reform yourself	**procures** pimps
a cord the hangman's rope/the	**powdered** using face powder (also
cord around the friar's waist	pickled, preserved)
tune fashion	**unshunned** inevitable
Trot old woman	

DUKE Fie, sirrah, a bawd, a wicked bawd!
       The evil that thou causest to be done,
       That is thy means to live. Do thou but think
       What 'tis to cram a maw or clothe a back
       From such a filthy vice; say to thyself,   20
       'From their abominable and beastly touches
       I drink, I eat, array myself, and live.'
       Canst thou believe thy living is a life,
       So stinkingly depending? Go mend, go mend.
POMPEY Indeed, it does stink in some sort, sir, but yet, sir, I would   25
    prove –
DUKE Nay, if the devil have given thee proofs for sin
       Thou wilt prove his. Take him to prison, officer,
       Correction and instruction must both work
       Ere this rude beast will profit.   30
ELBOW He must before the deputy, sir, he has given him warning:
    the deputy cannot abide a whoremaster. If he be a whoremonger
    and comes before him, he were as good go a mile on his errand.
DUKE That we were all, as some would seem to be,
       From our faults, as faults from seeming, free.   35

Enter LUCIO

ELBOW His neck will come to your waist, a cord, sir.
POMPEY I spy comfort, I cry bail: here's a gentleman and a friend of
    mine.
LUCIO How now, noble Pompey? What, at the wheels of Caesar? Art
    thou led in triumph? What, is there none of Pygmalion's images   40
    newly made woman to be had now, for putting the hand in the
    pocket and extracting it clutched? What reply, ha? What say'st
    thou to this tune, matter, and method? Is't not drowned i'th'last
    rain, ha? What say'st thou, Trot? Is the world as it was, man?
    Which is the way? Is it sad and few words? Or how? The trick of   45
    it?
DUKE Still thus, and thus: still worse.
LUCIO How doth my dear morsel, thy mistress? Procures she still,
    ha?
POMPEY Troth, sir, she hath eaten up all her beef, and she is herself   50
    in the tub.
LUCIO Why, 'tis good; it is the right of it; it must be so. Ever your
    fresh whore and your powdered bawd, an unshunned conse-
    quence; it must be so. Art going to prison, Pompey?
POMPEY Yes, faith, sir.   55

91

Pompey asks Lucio to stand bail for him, but Lucio refuses. Lucio complains that the Duke has left the country in Angelo's hands; he says that Angelo is applying the anti-lechery laws too strictly.

1 Lucio (in small groups)

Look carefully at the way Pompey addresses Lucio, and the way in which Lucio himself speaks to Pompey and the 'friar'. Discuss what this tells you about Lucio (for example, his social class, his attitudes, his education).

2 Lucio on stage

One director's idea of Lucio (opposite). What aspects of his character does the style of dress and posture highlight? In some cast lists, Lucio is described as 'a fantastic'. What do you think he would be called today?

husband housekeeper	**crabbed** harsh
wear fashion	**of a great kindred** belongs to a
steal from the state abdicate,	large family (everyone does it)
leave Vienna	**extirp** root out, eradicate
lenity lenience, mildness	

LUCIO Why, 'tis not amiss, Pompey. Farewell. Go say I sent thee thither. For debt, Pompey? Or how?

ELBOW For being a bawd, for being a bawd.

LUCIO Well then, imprison him: if imprisonment be the due of a bawd, why, 'tis his right. Bawd is he, doubtless, and of antiquity   60
too. Bawd born. Farewell, good Pompey. Commend me to the prison, Pompey; you will turn good husband now, Pompey, you will keep the house.

POMPEY I hope, sir, your good worship will be my bail.

LUCIO No indeed will I not, Pompey, it is not the wear. I will pray,   65
Pompey, to increase your bondage: if you take it not patiently, why, your mettle is the more. Adieu, trusty Pompey. – Bless you, friar.

DUKE And you.

LUCIO Does Bridget paint still, Pompey, ha?   70

ELBOW Come your ways, sir, come.

POMPEY You will not bail me then, sir?

LUCIO Then, Pompey, nor now. – What news abroad, friar? What news?

ELBOW Come your ways, sir, come.   75

LUCIO Go to kennel, Pompey, go. –

[*Exeunt Elbow, Pompey and Officers*]
What news, friar, of the Duke?

DUKE I know none. Can you tell me of any?

LUCIO Some say he is with the Emperor of Russia; other some he is in Rome; but where is he, think you?   80

DUKE I know not where, but wheresoever, I wish him well.

LUCIO It was a mad fantastical trick of him to steal from the state and usurp the beggary he was never born to. Lord Angelo dukes it well in his absence: he puts transgression to't.

DUKE He does well in't.   85

LUCIO A little more lenity to lechery would do no harm in him: something too crabbed that way, friar.

DUKE It is too general a vice, and severity must cure it.

LUCIO Yes, in good sooth, the vice is of a great kindred, it is well allied, but it is impossible to extirp it quite, friar, till eating and   90
drinking be put down. They say this Angelo was not made by man and woman after this downright way of creation: is it true, think you?

93

*Lucio comments mockingly on Angelo's unnatural coldness, and suggests that
the Duke had been a womaniser and a drinker. The 'friar' protests!*

---

1 A view of Angelo (in pairs)

On the previous page of script Lucio suggests that Angelo 'was not
made by man and woman . . .' (line 92) and proceeds to describe
Angelo using a variety of graphic images. Collect together all these
images, then choose the one which appeals to you most. Present that
image to the rest of the class, either through drama or by creating a
design on a sheet of a large paper. Guess which images each pair has
chosen, and discuss what Lucio's descriptions add to your perception
of Angelo.

2 Explore the comic possibilities (in groups of three)

Using lines 77–157, act out this encounter between Lucio and the
Duke in such a way as to bring out forcefully the comic and ironic
possibilities. The third member of the group acts as director, helping
to interpret the script and to translate it into action. Look out for
words which are capable of carrying double meanings – for example,
'sport' and 'service'. You might also find it useful to know that a
'codpiece' is a flap of clothing covering the male genitals, and that
'stockfishes' are dried cod.

3 'I know what I know' (line 131)

'Whenever anyone says "I know what I know", you know they are
lying', wrote one student. Do you agree with her? Why or why not?

---

motion generative male puppet
Ere before
your beggar of fifty an old
  beggarwoman
clack-dish a beggar's bowl
crotchets peculiarities
inward great friend

greater file the majority
subject people, population
unweighing undiscriminating
helmed steered
proclamation reputation
testimonied judged

DUKE How should he be made, then?

LUCIO Some report a sea-maid spawned him, some, that he was   95
    begot between two stock-fishes; but it is certain that when he
    makes water, his urine is congealed ice, that I know to be true;
    and he is a motion generative, that's infallible.

DUKE You are pleasant, sir, and speak apace.

LUCIO Why, what a ruthless thing is this in him, for the rebellion of a   100
    codpiece to take away the life of a man! Would the Duke that is
    absent have done this? Ere he would have hanged a man for the
    getting a hundred bastards, he would have paid for the nursing a
    thousand. He had some feeling of the sport, he knew the service,
    and that instructed him to mercy.   105

DUKE I never heard the absent Duke much detected for women, he
    was not inclined that way.

LUCIO Oh, sir, you are deceived.

DUKE 'Tis not possible.

LUCIO Who, not the Duke? Yes, your beggar of fifty: and his use   110
    was, to put a ducat in her clack-dish. The Duke had crotchets in
    him. He would be drunk too, that let me inform you.

DUKE You do him wrong, surely.

LUCIO Sir, I was an inward of his. A shy fellow was the Duke, and I
    believe I know the cause of his withdrawing.   115

DUKE What, I prithee, might be the cause?

LUCIO No, pardon: 'tis a secret must be locked within the teeth and
    the lips; but this I can let you understand: the greater file of the
    subject held the Duke to be wise.

DUKE Wise? Why, no question but he was.   120

LUCIO A very superficial, ignorant, unweighing fellow.

DUKE Either this is envy in you, folly, or mistaking. The very stream
    of his life and the business he hath helmed must, upon a
    warranted need, give him a better proclamation. Let him be but
    testimonied in his own bringings-forth and he shall appear to the   125
    envious a scholar, a statesman, and a soldier: therefore you speak
    unskilfully; or, if your knowledge be more, it is much darkened
    in your malice.

LUCIO Sir, I know him, and I love him.

DUKE Love talks with better knowledge, and knowledge with dearer   130
    love.

LUCIO Come, sir, I know what I know.

The 'friar' threatens to report Lucio's slanderous comments to the Duke. Lucio is unmoved, enquires after Claudio, then makes some final insults that cause the Duke to reflect on slander. Mistress Overdone pleads with Escalus for mercy.

1 Lucio's view of the Duke

Collect together all the comments Lucio makes about the Duke (lines 82–157). In this particular context, heavy with dramatic irony (see page 185), they can have great comic effect on stage. Consider, however, what evidence would indicate whether each of Lucio's suggestions has any foundation in truth or not. It will help you to copy out a list like the one below.

line	Lucio's comment	evidence?
82	'Mad fantastical trick'	sudden disappearance from Vienna
83	pretends to be a beggar ('usurp the beggary')	

2 Slander

The Duke is left to reflect on the fact that no one, however powerful, can escape slander. He clearly has in mind how Lucio has just slandered his own reputation (lines 158–61). Spend a few moments discussing with other students whether your points of view about slander are the same as the Duke's: is it 'back-wounding calumny' or legitimate criticism?

unhurtful an opposite harmless an enemy
filling a bottle with a tundish [funnel] having sexual intercourse
ungenitured sexless
continency restraint
untrussing dropping his trousers
eat mutton on Fridays disobey the rules of the Church
mouth with kiss
admonition warning
forfeit offend

DUKE I can hardly believe that, since you know not what you speak. But if ever the Duke return, as our prayers are he may, let me desire you to make your answer before him. If it be honest you 135 have spoke, you have courage to maintain it. I am bound to call upon you, and I pray you, your name?

LUCIO Sir, my name is Lucio, well known to the Duke.

DUKE He shall know you better, sir, if I may live to report you.

LUCIO I fear you not. 140

DUKE Oh, you hope the Duke will return no more? Or you imagine me too unhurtful an opposite? But indeed I can do you little harm: you'll forswear this again.

LUCIO I'll be hanged first. Thou art deceived in me, friar. But no more of this. Canst thou tell if Claudio die tomorrow, or no? 145

DUKE Why should he die, sir?

LUCIO Why? For filling a bottle with a tundish. I would the Duke we talk of were returned again. This ungenitured agent will unpeople the province with continency: sparrows must not build in his house eaves, because they are lecherous! The Duke yet 150 would have dark deeds darkly answered, he would never bring them to light. Would he were returned. Marry, this Claudio is condemned for untrussing. Farewell, good friar, I prithee pray for me. The Duke, I say to thee again, would eat mutton on Fridays. He's now past it, yet – and I say to thee – he would 155 mouth with a beggar though she smelt brown bread and garlic – say that I said so – farewell.   *Exit*

DUKE No might nor greatness in mortality
        Can censure 'scape: back-wounding calumny
        The whitest virtue strikes. What king so strong 160
        Can tie the gall up in the slanderous tongue?
        But who comes here?

Enter ESCALUS, PROVOST, MISTRESS OVERDONE [*and* OFFICERS]

ESCALUS Go, away with her to prison.

MISTRESS OVERDONE Good my lord, be good to me, your honour is accounted a merciful man – good my lord. 165

ESCALUS Double and treble admonition, and still forfeit in the same kind? This would make mercy swear and play the tyrant.

PROVOST A bawd of eleven years' continuance, may it please your honour.

Mistress Overdone has been accused of prostitution by Lucio. She claims that he has an illegitimate child. To the 'friar's' questions about the Duke's character and reputation, Escalus gives favourable replies.

1 Lucio the accuser

What effect does Mistress Overdone's revelation that it is Lucio who has made the accusation against her have on your opinion of Lucio? To help you remember what else Lucio has said about other characters, collect together some of his key comments. Copy the diagram below and add the comments.

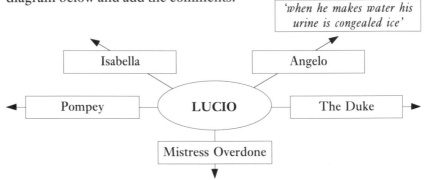

2 Escalus's opinion of the Duke (in pairs)

Escalus says that the Duke 'above all other strifes contended especially to know himself' (lines 199–200). From your knowledge of the Duke, discuss how appropriate you find this description. Contrast Lucio's earlier comments on the Duke with those now given by Escalus. Take some notes, then feed back your findings to the rest of the class (including what light the remark sheds on Escalus himself).

3 'Novelty is only in request' (in small groups)

Fashion and change are all that matter, and money ruins friendship, says the Duke in lines 192–6. Is this true today?

Philip and Jacob A feast-day in May
furnished with divines provided with priests
wrought by my pity administered justice with my mercy

the See Rome, the diocese presided over by the Pope (his holiness)
undertaking enterprise
security foolish confidence
lent him visitation visited him

MISTRESS OVERDONE My lord, this is one Lucio's information 170
    against me. Mistress Kate Keepdown was with child by him in
    the Duke's time, he promised her marriage, his child is a year
    and a quarter old come Philip and Jacob – I have kept it myself –
    and see how he goes about to abuse me.
ESCALUS That fellow is a fellow of much licence: let him be called 175
    before us. Away with her to prison, go to, no more words.
                [Exeunt Officers with Mistress Overdone]
    Provost, my brother Angelo will not be altered, Claudio must die
    tomorrow. Let him be furnished with divines, and have all
    charitable preparation. If my brother wrought by my pity, it
    should not be so with him. 180
PROVOST So please you, this friar hath been with him, and advised
    him for th'entertainment of death.
ESCALUS Good even, good father.
DUKE Bliss and goodness on you.
ESCALUS Of whence are you? 185
DUKE Not of this country, though my chance is now
        To use it for my time. I am a brother
        Of gracious order, late come from the See,
        In special business from his holiness.
ESCALUS What news abroad i'th'world? 190
DUKE None but that there is so great a fever on goodness that the
    dissolution of it must cure it. Novelty is only in request, and it is
    as dangerous to be aged in any kind of course, as it is virtuous to
    be constant in any undertaking. There is scarce truth enough
    alive to make societies secure, but security enough to make 195
    fellowships accursed. Much upon this riddle runs the wisdom of
    the world. This news is old enough, yet it is every day's news. I
    pray you, sir, of what disposition was the Duke?
ESCALUS One that above all other strifes contended especially to
    know himself. 200
DUKE What pleasure was he given to?
ESCALUS Rather rejoicing to see another merry, than merry at
    anything which professed to make him rejoice. A gentleman of
    all temperance. But leave we him to his events, with a prayer they
    may prove prosperous, and let me desire to know how you find 205
    Claudio prepared. I am made to understand that you have lent
    him visitation.

*The Duke tells Escalus that Claudio is prepared for death. Escalus reveals
that he has tried to change Angelo's mind, but failed. Left alone, the
Duke reflects on Angelo's hypocrisy.*

1 The Duke's soliloquy (in groups of ten to twenty-two)

There is a noticeable shift in language style at line 223 when the
Duke is left alone on the stage to muse about Angelo's actions. He
speaks in a series of short rhyming couplets. Organise yourselves into
a double circle or line, in pairs. Each pair should take and memorise
at least a couplet each, so that the whole speech is divided up between
the whole group. Experiment with ways of presenting the speech – for
example using balancing movements, weighing one student against
another.

After you have tried various physical ways of enacting the words,
discuss what you notice about the structure and content of the Duke's
speech.

2 Tableau a couplet (in small groups of three or four)

Choose any of the couplets at
lines 223–4, or 237–8, or 242–3.
Find ways of presenting them to
the rest of the class in the form of
a tableau.

3 The Duke

'He who the sword of heaven will
bear/Should be as holy, as severe.'

---

sinister unjust
yet had . . . die he made up false
  reasons for living, but I have
  convinced him it is best to die
shore limit
answer measure up to

straitness absolute strictness
Pattern . . . go be a model of
  uprightness and goodness
weed dig out
draw deceive
false exacting deceitful demands

DUKE He professes to have received no sinister measure from his
judge, but most willingly humbles himself to the determination
of justice; yet had he framed to himself, by the instruction of his   210
frailty, many deceiving promises of life, which I by my good
leisure have discredited to him; and now is he resolved to die.

ESCALUS You have paid the heavens your function, and the prisoner
the very debt of your calling. I have laboured for the poor gentleman to the extremest shore of my modesty, but my brother   215
justice have I found so severe that he hath forced me to tell him
he is indeed Justice.

DUKE If his own life answer the straitness of his proceeding, it shall
become him well; wherein if he chance to fail, he hath sentenced
himself.   220

ESCALUS I am going to visit the prisoner. Fare you well.

DUKE Peace be with you.

                          [Exeunt Escalus and Provost]

    He who the sword of heaven will bear
    Should be as holy, as severe:
    Pattern in himself to know,   225
    Grace to stand, and virtue go:
    More, nor less to others paying
    Than by self-offences weighing.
    Shame to him, whose cruel striking
    Kills for faults of his own liking.   230
    Twice treble shame on Angelo,
    To weed my vice, and let his grow.
    Oh, what may man within him hide,
    Though angel on the outward side?
    How may likeness made in crimes,   235
    Making practice on the times,
    To draw with idle spiders' strings
    Most ponderous and substantial things?
    Craft against vice I must apply.
    With Angelo tonight shall lie   240
    His old betrothèd but despised;
    So disguise shall by th'disguised
    Pay with falsehood false exacting
    And perform an old contracting.   *Exit*

Looking back at Act 3
Activities for groups or individuals

1 ''Tis best thou diest quickly'

Isabella's reaction to her brother's pleas (Scene 1, line 151) has been read by different critics in quite opposing ways, as the following readings show. Can you suggest which were proposed by men and which by women? Explain why.

- Isabella is neurotic about sex.
- She is unnaturally cold and unfeeling.
- Psychologically, Isabella is denying her latent sexual attraction towards Angelo.
- Isabella has the right to decide what happens to her own body, and she is merely upholding that principle.
- If Isabella gives way to Angelo's demands, what chance has *any* woman in Vienna?

2 Angelo: appearance and reality

Angelo is described by Isabella as an 'outward-sainted deputy' who 'is yet a devil' (3.1.88–91). Even his name suggests the appearance of an 'angel'. Isabella tells of Angelo's 'devilish mercy' (3.1.64) and suggests that he dresses in the 'cunning livery of hell'. This notion of Angelo as angel-devil is reiterated by the Duke:

'Oh, what may man within him hide,
Though angel on the outward side?' (3.2.233–4)

Find ways of presenting a series of 'portraits' of Angelo accompanied by relevant quotations from the play so far. For your 'portraits' you could make use of mime, tableaux, choral speech. Choose four moments from the play, and focus on the idea of the outwardly angelic man hiding the devil beneath.

3 Gossip column

Rumours about the absent Duke are likely to spread around Vienna. Imagine that Lucio writes a gossip column (under a pen-name) for the popular weekly scandal-sheet, *The Vienna Eye*. What might he be penning for this week's publication?

4 Isabella's dilemma

Look at these three photographs, and identify the male character pictured with Isabella in each case.

Using only lines selected from the play so far, explore the dilemma that faces Isabella and the pressure she is under from the three powerful male characters in her life. How does each man assert his power over her? Share your ideas with the rest of the class.

5 Palace statement (in pairs)

The Duke's press secretary has to counter speculation and make an official statement explaining the absence of the Duke and the choice of Angelo as deputy. Write or record on tape a series of such press statements, taking account of new developments in Act 3.

The Duke visits Mariana, who is listening to sad music. When Isabella arrives, Mariana leaves her and the Duke to talk together in private.

---

1 The song – is it Shakespeare's? (in pairs)

'Shakespeare scholars' disagree about whether the song and the dialogue up to line 23 were actually written by Shakespeare. In some productions, directors omit these lines. If you were directing a production of the play, would you include the song and subsequent dialogue or not? Give your reasons.

2 Mariana at the moated grange

The nineteenth-century poet Tennyson was inspired by the romantic image of Mariana. He composed a poem called 'Mariana' based on the jilted lover pining for Angelo 'at the moated grange'. Look at the photograph below. Is that how you imagine her to be? What particular atmosphere is established by the director? Talk together about the expectations you have of Mariana.

---

brawling disturbing
much upon this time just about
  now

constantly absolutely
crave your forbearance ask you to
  leave

ACT 4   SCENE 1
The moated grange

Enter MARIANA, *and* BOY *singing*

BOY [*Sings*] Take, oh take those lips away,
    That so sweetly were forsworn,
  And those eyes, the break of day,
    Lights that do mislead the morn;
  But my kisses bring again, bring again,   5
  Seals of love, but sealed in vain, sealed in vain.

Enter DUKE [*disguised as a friar*]

MARIANA Break off thy song and haste thee quick away.
  Here comes a man of comfort, whose advice
  Hath often stilled my brawling discontent. –
                       [*Exit Boy*]
  I cry you mercy, sir, and well could wish   10
  You had not found me here so musical.
  Let me excuse me, and believe me so,
  My mirth it much displeased, but pleased my woe.
DUKE 'Tis good; though music oft hath such a charm
  To make bad good and good provoke to harm.   15
  I pray you tell me, hath anybody enquired for me here today?
  Much upon this time have I promised here to meet.
MARIANA You have not been enquired after: I have sat here all day.

Enter ISABELLA

DUKE I do constantly believe you. The time is come even now. I shall
  crave your forbearance a little, may be I will call upon you anon 20
  for some advantage to yourself.
MARIANA I am always bound to you.   *Exit*

Isabella gives the Duke details of her secret night-time rendezvous with Angelo. The Duke allows Isabella time to speak to Mariana in private.

---

1 'This "good" deputy' (in small groups)

Spend five minutes discussing how you think the Duke is using the word 'good' in this context (line 24). It could be deliberately respectful, mindful of Angelo's high position in society; or it might be used with heavily ironic emphasis. How will Isabella respond to the different interpretations of 'good'?

2 Mime Angelo's instructions (in pairs)

Isabella says that Angelo gave her the instructions for the rendezvous 'in action all of precept' (accompanied by gestures). Mime this scene between Angelo and Isabella, taking care to make all significant gestures clearly pronounced. Show your mime to the rest of the class.

3 The 'bed-trick' (in groups of three)

The Duke himself does not inform Mariana of the 'bed-trick'; he leaves that delicate task to Isabella. Discuss whether you think that is because:

- he realises it is better coming from another woman
- he is sensitive to Mariana's finer feelings
- he is a moral coward and gets other people to do his dirty work for him
- some other reason (what?).

4 What do they say? (in groups of three)

Improvise the conversation that is about to take place between the two women. The third member of the group can help with giving ideas and directions.

---

circummured with brick surrounded by a brick wall
planchèd made of wooden planks
tane taken
concerning her observance important to her to observe

a repair i'th' dark going to the place after dark
possessed him explained to him
my most stay the longest possible time I can stay

DUKE Very well met, and welcome.
What is the news from this good deputy?
ISABELLA He hath a garden circummured with brick,   25
Whose western side is with a vineyard backed;
And to that vineyard is a planchèd gate
That makes his opening with this bigger key.
This other doth command a little door
Which from the vineyard to the garden leads;   30
There have I made my promise, upon the heavy
Middle of the night to call upon him.
DUKE But shall you on your knowledge find this way?
ISABELLA I have tane a duc and wary note upon't.
With whispering and most guilty diligence   35
In action all of precept, he did show me
The way twice o'er.
DUKE   Are there no other tokens
Between you 'greed, concerning her observance?
ISABELLA No, none, but only a repair i'th'dark
And that I have possessed him my most stay   40
Can be but brief: for I have made him know
I have a servant comes with me along
That stays upon me, whose persuasion is
I come about my brother.
DUKE   'Tis well borne up.
I have not yet made known to Mariana   45
A word of this. What ho, within, come forth.

Enter MARIANA

I pray you be acquainted with this maid,
She comes to do you good.
ISABELLA   I do desire the like.
DUKE Do you persuade yourself that I respect you?
MARIANA Good friar, I know you do, and have found it.   50
DUKE Take then this your companion by the hand,
Who hath a story ready for your ear.
I shall attend your leisure, but make haste:
The vaporous night approaches.
MARIANA [*To Isabella*] Will't please you walk aside?   55
[*Mariana and Isabella walk aside*]

Mariana agrees to the 'bed-trick'. The Duke assures her that no sin will be committed, since Angelo and she are already technically contracted to be married.

1 'If you advise it' (in pairs or groups of three)

Both women appear to have unshakeable trust in the 'friar'. They entrust their whole futures, their chastities even, to this man. Consider the following suggestions in turn and discuss why you think that the women are so compliant:

- in the society of the play, women naturally defer to male authority
- in Jacobean England, women would naturally defer to male authority, therefore Shakespeare is making that assumption here
- it is because the man is a friar, a holy man
- both Isabella and Mariana are presented as acquiescent and passive; they don't have minds of their own
- it always takes a man to get women properly organised
- some other reason.

Compare your 'reading' of this situation with those of other groups. Discuss the range of interpretations. Can you analyse why particular members of your class read the scene in different ways?

2 The Duke's soliloquy

'It's just like Royalty and politicians and the popular press and television. It exactly describes what happens today', said one student about lines 56–61. To test the truth of her claim, collect examples from newspapers and magazines, and caption them with phrases from the Duke's soliloquy.

---

place and greatness people with high status
false and most contrarious quest treacherous and lying reporting

escapes of wit irresponsible jokes
rack tear apart
sith since
flourish attractively cover
tithe seed

DUKE   Oh place and greatness, millions of false eyes
　　　　Are stuck upon thee; volumes of report
　　　　Run with these false and most contrarious quest
　　　　Upon thy doings; thousand escapes of wit
　　　　Make thee the father of their idle dream   60
　　　　And rack thee in their fancies.
　　　　　　MARIANA *and* ISABELLA [*approach the Duke*]
　　　　Welcome, how agreed?
ISABELLA   She'll take the enterprise upon her, father,
　　　　If you advise it.
DUKE   　　　　　　　　It is not my consent,
　　　　But my entreaty too.
ISABELLA   　　　　　　　　Little have you to say   65
　　　　When you depart from him but, soft and low,
　　　　'Remember now my brother.'
MARIANA   　　　　　　　　　　Fear me not.
DUKE   Nor, gentle daughter, fear you not at all.
　　　　He is your husband on a pre-contract:
　　　　To bring you thus together 'tis no sin,   70
　　　　Sith that the justice of your title to him
　　　　Doth flourish the deceit. Come, let us go,
　　　　Our corn's to reap, for yet our tithe's to sow.
　　　　　　　　　　　　　　　　　　　　　Exeunt

The Provost offers Pompey freedom if he will act as assistant to Abhorson, the hangman. Abhorson is not impressed by Pompey.

1 Law and morality (in small groups)

In Vienna, pimping is illegal, sex outside of marriage is illegal, but cutting a man's head off or hanging him is legal. Pompey cheerfully goes from being 'an unlawful bawd' to 'a lawful hangman'. Talk together about the relationship of the law to notions of morality in the play.

Pompey in the prison.

2 What's in a name?

For an activity on Abhorson's name, see page 42.

---

sirrah fellow (used to address a subordinate)
snatches puns, word-plays
gyves fetters, shackles
unpitied pitiless
meet appropriate

compound . . . year agree an annual wage
plead his estimation make claims for a pay rise
mystery profession

ACT 4   SCENE 2
The prison   The Provost's room

Enter PROVOST and POMPEY

PROVOST Come hither, sirrah; can you cut off a man's head?

POMPEY If the man be a bachelor, sir, I can; but if he be a married man, he's his wife's head, and I can never cut off a woman's head.

PROVOST Come, sir, leave me your snatches and yield me a direct   5
answer. Tomorrow morning are to die Claudio and Barnardine. Here is in our prison a common executioner, who in his office lacks a helper. If you will take it on you to assist him, it shall redeem you from your gyves. If not, you shall have your full time of imprisonment, and your deliverance with an unpitied whipping;   10
for you have been a notorious bawd.

POMPEY Sir, I have been an unlawful bawd time out of mind, but yet I will be content to be a lawful hangman: I would be glad to receive some instruction from my fellow partner.

PROVOST What ho, Abhorson! Where's Abhorson, there?   15

Enter ABHORSON

ABHORSON Do you call, sir?

PROVOST Sirrah, here's a fellow will help you tomorrow in your execution. If you think it meet, compound with him by the year and let him abide here with you; if not, use him for the present and dismiss him, he cannot plead his estimation with you: he   20
hath been a bawd.

ABHORSON A bawd, sir? Fie upon him, he will discredit our mystery!

PROVOST Go to, sir, you weigh equally: a feather will turn the scale.

Exit

Abhorson defends the occupation of hangman. Pompey agrees to serve as his assistant. The Provost tells Claudio he must be executed tomorrow. Barnardine, also to die, is still asleep.

1 Show the image (in groups of three)

Pompey says that Abhorson has 'a hanging look' (line 25). Show each other what you think that might look like.

2 A mystery

Abhorson claims that hanging is a highly skilled trade, a 'mystery', or sacred rite available only to a few selected people. He 'proves' it with lines 34–7 (which, because Shakespeare's words were jumbled or missed out by the first printer in 1623, don't quite make sense). Write four lines of your own to substitute for lines 34–7 to 'prove' that the job of hangman is a 'mystery'.

A public hanging (from a contemporary wood cut).

3 Frozen moment (in pairs)

Take the Provost's line 'here's the warrant, Claudio, for thy death' (line 50) and freeze that moment as if on stage. Discuss how it might be said, and how Claudio might react. Share your 'frozen moment' with the rest of the class.

---

favour permission or face
using painting using make-up
apparel clothing (the hangman was entitled to claim the clothes of his victim)

true honest
penitent trade forgiving job
yare ready

POMPEY Pray, sir, by your good favour – for surely, sir, a good favour
you have, but that you have a hanging look – do you call, sir, your   25
occupation a mystery?

ABHORSON Ay, sir, a mystery.

POMPEY Painting, sir, I have heard say, is a mystery; and your
whores, sir, being members of my occupation, using painting, do
prove my occupation a mystery; but what mystery there should   30
be in hanging, if I should be hanged, I cannot imagine.

ABHORSON Sir, it is a mystery.

POMPEY Proof.

ABHORSON Every true man's apparel fits your thief. If it be too little
for your thief, your true man thinks it big enough. If it be too big   35
for your thief, your thief thinks it little enough: so every true
man's apparel fits your thief.

Enter PROVOST

PROVOST Are you agreed?

POMPEY Sir, I will serve him, for I do find your hangman is a more
penitent trade than your bawd: he doth oftener ask forgiveness.   40

PROVOST You, sirrah, provide your block and your axe tomorrow,
four a clock.

ABHORSON Come on, bawd, I will instruct thee in my trade. Follow.

POMPEY I do desire to learn, sir, and I hope, if you have occasion to
use me for your own turn, you shall find me yare. For truly, sir,   45
for your kindness, I owe you a good turn.

PROVOST Call hither Barnardine and Claudio.

Exeunt [Abhorson and Pompey]

Th'one has my pity; not a jot the other,
Being a murderer, though he were my brother.

Enter CLAUDIO

Look, here's the warrant, Claudio, for thy death.   50
'Tis now dead midnight, and by eight tomorrow
Thou must be made immortal. Where's Barnardine?

CLAUDIO As fast locked up in sleep as guiltless labour
When it lies starkly in the traveller's bones.
He will not wake.

*The Provost tells Claudio to prepare himself for execution. The Duke argues
that Angelo's personality and actions match each other. Loud knocking
is heard at the portal gate.*

1 'It is a bitter deputy'

As you read through the play, collect together descriptions of Angelo.
(You may already have made a collection through the activity on page
94.) What difference does it make to you as a reader or as a spectator
whether the comments are made by those who know Angelo per-
sonally or those – like the Provost – who have had little personal
contact?

2 Angelo: appearance and reality (in groups of five or six)

Divide up lines 66–72 into smaller sense units. Every group member
takes and learns one unit each. Work out a way of presenting the lines
so that the irony of the words is brought out. You could employ mime,
tableaux, choral reading or any other drama technique in your
presentation.

3 Dramatic effect (in groups of three or four)

Shakespeare uses the sound of knocking at doors to great dramatic
effect in several plays (*Macbeth, Romeo and Juliet, King Richard II*).
Talk together about the effect of the repeated knocking off-stage, and
the accompanying comments about last-minute reprieves in this
section of the scene.

Now improvise a short play called 'The Knock at the Door'.
Concentrate on ways of raising dramatic tension as the scene
progresses.

---

curfew evening bell
stroke and line stroke of the
  executioner's axe, and the line of
  the hangman's cord (or signing
  official orders)

qualify put an end to
mealed stained
steelèd iron-hearted
unsisting postern unyielding back
  door

PROVOST   Who can do good on him?   55
     Well, go, prepare yourself –
           [*Knocking within*]
                   But hark, what noise?
     Heaven give your spirits comfort.
                       [*Exit Claudio*]
           [*Knocking within*]
                  By and by!
     I hope it is some pardon or reprieve
     For the most gentle Claudio.

        Enter DUKE [*disguised as a friar*]

                 Welcome, father.
DUKE The best and wholesom'st spirits of the night   60
     Envelop you, good provost: who called here of late?
PROVOST None since the curfew rung.
DUKE Not Isabel?
PROVOST   No.
DUKE   They will then, ere't be long.
PROVOST What comfort is for Claudio?
DUKE There's some in hope.
PROVOST   It is a bitter deputy.   65
DUKE Not so, not so: his life is paralleled
     Even with the stroke and line of his great justice:
     He doth with holy abstinence subdue
     That in himself which he spurs on his power
     To qualify in others. Were he mealed with that   70
     Which he corrects, then were he tyrannous;
     But this being so, he's just.
           [*Knocking within*]
                     [*Exit Provost*]
                Now are they come.
     This is a gentle provost; seldom when
     The steelèd gaoler is the friend of men.
           [*Knocking within*]
     How now, what noise? That spirit's possessed with haste   75
     That wounds th'unsisting postern with these strokes.

The Provost does not believe that Claudio will be pardoned. A messenger
brings Angelo's note. The Duke secretly expects it to be a reprieve.
He asks the Provost to read it out.

1 The offender pardons the offence (in groups of five)

a Make a series of tableaux to illustrate the Duke's aside:

'This is his pardon, purchased by such sin
For which the pardoner himself is in.' (lines 94–5)

b The Duke develops his idea in a second couplet (lines 96–7). Try
to explain in your own words what you think he means by this.
Suggest some parallel situations about people in high places from
today's news stories.

c The Duke claims that 'When vice makes mercy, mercy's so
extended/That for the fault's love is th'offender friended.' Discuss
what you think the Duke means by that. Do you agree with the
Duke's sentiments about sin and mercy? Talk together about the
way other 'sins' are dealt with in the play.

2 What's in the note?

If you haven't seen or read the play before, try guessing what Angelo's
note says!

3 The Messenger

This is the Messenger's only appearance. Imagine that it is your first
stage role. How will you prepare for and perform it?

countermand reprieve	**remiss** slack, neglectful
siege of justice seat of judgement	**unwonted putting on** unusual
celerity speed	demand
belike I suppose	

[Enter PROVOST]

PROVOST There he must stay until the officer
          Arrives to let him in: he is called up.
DUKE Have you no countermand for Claudio yet
          But he must die tomorrow?
PROVOST   None, sir, none.   80
DUKE As near the dawning, provost, as it is,
          You shall hear more ere morning.
PROVOST   Happily
          You something know; yet I believe there comes
          No countermand. No such example have we.
          Besides, upon the very siege of justice   85
          Lord Angelo hath to the public ear
          Professed the contrary.

                    Enter a MESSENGER

                              This is his lordship's man.
DUKE And here comes Claudio's pardon.
MESSENGER My lord hath sent you this note, and by me this further
          charge – that you swerve not from the smallest article of it,   90
          neither in time, matter, or other circumstance. Good morrow:
          for, as I take it, it is almost day.
PROVOST I shall obey him.
                                            [Exit Messenger]
DUKE *[Aside]* This is his pardon, purchased by such sin
          For which the pardoner himself is in.   95
          Hence hath offence his quick celerity,
          When it is borne in high authority.
          When vice makes mercy, mercy's so extended
          That for the fault's love is th'offender friended.
          Now, sir, what news?   100
PROVOST I told you: Lord Angelo, belike, thinking me remiss in
          mine office, awakens me with this unwonted putting on,
          methinks strangely: for he hath not used it before.
DUKE Pray you, let's hear.

Angelo's note orders Claudio's execution and demands that Claudio's head be delivered to him afterwards. The Duke asks the Provost to do him a dangerous favour.

1 Asides (in pairs)

One partner reads out the letter (lines 105–10), pausing after each sentence. In those pauses, the other partner interjects the Duke's thoughts as if they were asides.

2 Improvise a scene (in groups of about four)

Barnardine is described as 'insensible of mortality and desperately mortal', and the Provost gives other aspects of his character in lines 125–34. Imagine what the man who is described in the above terms might be like.

Improvise the scene where Barnardine was first imprisoned. What crime do you think he has committed?

3 What is the Duke's plan?

If you do not know the story, can you guess what the Duke's plan is going to be? Jot some ideas down on paper. See if you guessed correctly when you turn the page!

Bohemian Bohemia is part of the former Czechoslovakia
nine years old for nine years
fact crime
touched affected
apprehends imagines, anticipates

wants advice needs spiritual direction
lay myself in hazard take a risk
manifested effect clear demonstration
present immediate

PROVOST [*Reading*] *the letter* 'Whatsoever you may hear to the   105
contrary, let Claudio be executed by four of the clock, and in the
afternoon, Barnardine. For my better satisfaction let me have
Claudio's head sent me by five. Let this be duly performed with
a thought that more depends on it than we must yet deliver.
Thus fail not to do your office, as you will answer it at your peril.'   110
– What say you to this, sir?

DUKE What is that Barnardine who is to be executed in th'afternoon?

PROVOST A Bohemian born, but here nursed up and bred; one that
is a prisoner nine years old.

DUKE How came it that the absent Duke had not either delivered   115
him to his liberty or executed him? I have heard it was ever his
manner to do so.

PROVOST His friends still wrought reprieves for him: and indeed his
fact, till now in the government of Lord Angelo, came not to an
undoubtful proof.   120

DUKE It is now apparent?

PROVOST Most manifest, and not denied by himself.

DUKE Hath he borne himself penitently in prison? How seems he to
be touched?

PROVOST A man that apprehends death no more dreadfully but as a   125
drunken sleep: careless, reckless, and fearless of what's past,
present, or to come: insensible of mortality and desperately
mortal.

DUKE He wants advice.

PROVOST He will hear none. He hath evermore had the liberty of the   130
prison: give him leave to escape hence, he would not. Drunk
many times a day, if not many days entirely drunk. We have very
oft awaked him, as if to carry him to execution, and showed him
a seeming warrant for it. It hath not moved him at all.

DUKE More of him anon. There is written in your brow, provost,   135
honesty and constancy; if I read it not truly, my ancient skill
beguiles me; but in the boldness of my cunning, I will lay myself
in hazard. Claudio, whom here you have warrant to execute, is
no greater forfeit to the law than Angelo who hath sentenced
him. To make you understand this in a manifested effect, I crave   140
but four days' respite: for the which, you are to do me both a
present and a dangerous courtesy.

The Duke proposes sending Barnardine's head to Angelo in place of Claudio's. The Provost is fearful, but the 'friar' reassures him by producing a letter bearing the Duke's signature.

1 What is in the letters?

Several letters are mentioned by the Duke in lines 172–83. One he shows to the Provost. The others, which Angelo is about to receive, are 'of strange tenor'. Write the letter the 'friar' gives to the Provost, and write two other letters which Angelo might receive.

2 The Duke's seal

The disguised Duke shows the Provost a signet ring to prove his authority. This ring, the 'seal of the Duke', would bear a picture or emblem symbolic of Duke Vincentio.

Design the Duke's seal. Ensure that it unmistakeably represents the ruler of Vienna.

3 What if . . .? (in pairs or groups of three)

What if the Provost doesn't trust the 'friar' and goes ahead with Claudio's execution? How will the story continue?

4 But why?

Why doesn't the Duke simply take the Provost into his complete confidence and reduce the risk of his plot going wrong?

---

cross disobey
order brotherhood of friars
tie the beard trim and tidy it up
avouch uphold
coat friar's habit
hand handwriting

character handwriting
tenor sense
unfolding star the morning star (when sheep are released from their folds)
shrift confession

PROVOST Pray, sir, in what?

DUKE In the delaying death.

PROVOST Alack, how may I do it? Having the hour limited, and an   145
express command, under penalty, to deliver his head in the view
of Angelo? I may make my case as Claudio's to cross this in the
smallest.

DUKE By the vow of mine order I warrant you. If my instructions may
be your guide, let this Barnardine be this morning executed and   150
his head borne to Angelo.

PROVOST Angelo hath seen them both and will discover the favour.

DUKE Oh, death's a great disguiser, and you may add to it: shave the
head and tie the beard, and say it was the desire of the penitent
to be so bared before his death. You know the course is common.   155
If anything fall to you upon this, more than thanks and good
fortune, by the saint whom I profess I will plead against it with
my life.

PROVOST Pardon me, good father, it is against my oath.

DUKE Were you sworn to the Duke or to the deputy?   160

PROVOST To him, and to his substitutes.

DUKE You will think you have made no offence, if the Duke avouch
the justice of your dealing?

PROVOST But what likelihood is in that?

DUKE Not a resemblance, but a certainty; yet since I see you fearful,   165
that neither my coat, integrity, nor persuasion, can with ease
attempt you, I will go further than I meant, to pluck all fears out
of you: look you, sir, here is the hand and seal of the Duke. You
know the character I doubt not, and the signet is not strange to
you.   170

PROVOST I know them both.

DUKE The contents of this is the return of the Duke; you shall anon
over-read it at your pleasure, where you shall find within these
two days he will be here. This is a thing that Angelo knows not,
for he this very day receives letters of strange tenor, perchance of   175
the Duke's death, perchance entering into some monastery, but
by chance nothing of what is writ. Look, th'unfolding star calls
up the shepherd. Put not yourself into amazement how these
things should be: all difficulties are but easy when they are
known. Call your executioner, and off with Barnardine's head. I   180
will give him a present shrift, and advise him for a better place.
Yet you are amazed, but this shall absolutely resolve you. Come
away, it is almost clear dawn.

[*Exeunt*]

Pompey describes the prison inmates and their crimes. Abhorson orders Pompey to fetch Barnardine and prepare him for execution.

1 Meet the gang (in groups of about ten)

In lines 1–16 Pompey describes his fellow prisoners, old friends from the brothel. One person takes the part of Pompey, the rest of the group choose an inmate each. As each prisoner is introduced by Pompey in turn, mime an action to suit the name.

You might need some help interpreting all of the names and the various 'occupations' – but don't be afraid to use your imagination!

- Rash – reckless (with a play on 'rash', a smooth-finished cloth)
- Caper – a very fashionable high-kicking dance step
- Three-pile – velvet
- Dizie – dizzy, foolish (or possibly 'dice' used for gambling)
- Deepvow – a heavy swearer
- Copperspur – simulating gold
- Starvelackey – he cannot or will not pay his servant
- Dropheir – a gallant living off the money of wealthy young men (heirs), pimping for them and swindling them
- Pudding – dull and stupid
- Forthright – a thrust of a lance at full tilt on horseback
- Shoetie – men's shoes were tied with immensely long ribbons, arranged into very ornate rosettes and bows
- Halfcan – 'Halfpint' (a small person); a can was a full measure of beer
- Pots – pot-boy (working in a pub).

With 'the rapier and dagger man', 'the tilter', 'stabbed Pots', Shakespeare may have had in mind the increase in brawling on the streets of London amongst 'roaring boys'. This was strictly prohibited and punished under the 'Statute of Stabbing' (1604).

---

house of profession brothel
ginger chewed by old women (and thought to be an aphrodisiac)
mercer dealer in fabrics
peaches impeaches, denounces
doers fornicators
'for the Lord's sake' the cry of prisoners begging for charity

ACT 4 SCENE 3
The prison

Enter POMPEY

POMPEY I am as well acquainted here as I was in our house of
profession. One would think it were Mistress Overdone's own
house, for here be many of her old customers. First, here's
young Master Rash, he's in for a commodity of brown paper and
old ginger, nine score and seventeen pounds, of which he made   5
five marks ready money: marry, then ginger was not much
in request, for the old women were all dead. Then is there
here one Master Caper, at the suit of Master Threepile the
mercer, for some four suits of peach-coloured satin, which now
'peaches him a beggar. Then have we here young Dizie, and   10
young Master Deepvow, and Master Copperspur, and Master
Starvelackey the rapier and dagger man, and young Dropheir
that killed lusty Pudding, and Master Forthright the tilter, and
brave Master Shoetie the great traveller, and wild Halfcan that
stabbed Pots, and I think forty more, all great doers in our trade,   15
and are now 'for the Lord's sake'.

Enter ABHORSON

ABHORSON Sirrah, bring Barnardine hither.
POMPEY Master Barnardine, you must rise and be hanged, Master
Barnardine!
ABHORSON What ho, Barnardine!   20
BARNARDINE [*Within*] A pox o'your throats, who makes that noise
there? What are you?
POMPEY Your friends, sir, the hangman: You must be so good, sir, to
rise and be put to death.
BARNARDINE [*Within*] Away, you rogue, away, I am sleepy.   25
ABHORSON Tell him he must awake, and that quickly, too.
POMPEY Pray, Master Barnardine, awake till you are executed, and
sleep afterwards.
ABHORSON Go in to him, and fetch him out.
POMPEY He is coming, sir, he is coming, I hear his straw rustle.   30

Barnardine refuses to prepare himself for death. The Duke arrives and tries to persuade him, but also fails.

1 Humour in hanging? (in small groups)

Directors and actors often seize upon the lines opposite to present an intensely comic scene in which the entry of Barnardine is a memorable moment. Talk together about the types of humour present in the scene. These might include:

- dramatic irony
- word-play
- surreal humour
- visual humour
- irony
- farce
- comic incongruity
- other forms of comedy.

Then act out the lines.

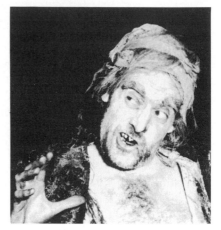

Barnardine puts in an appearance in the Royal Shakespeare Company's 1962 production.

2 'Unmeet for death' (in pairs)

Perhaps it seems strange today that the Duke, the Provost and the hangman would not contemplate executing a man who was not in the right religious frame of mind for death. Before execution a condemned man would make confession before a priest and prepare his soul for death. Because Barnardine is unrepentant (he's drunk) he refuses to co-operate with the frustrated trio. Spend five minutes talking together about the attitudes of each of the characters on stage to death. Contrast them with your recollections of Claudio's attitude.

clap into get on with quickly	**ward** cell
betimes quickly, early	**gravel heart** hard heart
ghostly spiritual	**unmeet** unfitted
billets thick wooden sticks	**transport** execute

Enter BARNARDINE

ABHORSON Is the axe upon the block, sirrah?

POMPEY Very ready, sir.

BARNARDINE How now, Abhorson, what's the news with you?

ABHORSON Truly, sir, I would desire you to clap into your prayers; for look you, the warrant's come.   35

BARNARDINE You rogue, I have been drinking all night, I am not fitted for't.

POMPEY Oh, the better, sir; for he that drinks all night, and is hanged betimes in the morning, may sleep the sounder all the next day.   40

Enter DUKE [*disguised as a friar*]

ABHORSON Look you, sir, here comes your ghostly father, do we jest now, think you?

DUKE Sir, induced by my charity, and hearing how hastily you are to depart, I am come to advise you, comfort you, and pray with you.

BARNARDINE Friar, not I. I have been drinking hard all night, and I   45
will have more time to prepare me, or they shall beat out my brains with billets. I will not consent to die this day, that's certain.

DUKE Oh, sir, you must; and therefore I beseech you
Look forward on the journey you shall go.   50

BARNARDINE I swear I will not die today for any man's persuasion.

DUKE But hear you –

BARNARDINE Not a word. If you have anything to say to me, come to my ward, for thence will not I today.   *Exit*

Enter PROVOST

DUKE Unfit to live or die: oh gravel heart!   55
After him, fellows, bring him to the block.
[*Exeunt Abhorson and Pompey*]

PROVOST Now, sir, how do you find the prisoner?

DUKE A creature unprepared, unmeet for death,
And to transport him, in the mind he is,
Were damnable.

The Provost suggests substituting the head of another prisoner who died that morning. The Duke eagerly agrees. He decides to write to Angelo to arrange a public homecoming.

---

1 'An accident that heaven provides'? (in pairs)

Very different interpretations exist of the Duke's claim at line 68 that God is on his side. Consider each suggested 'reading' of the line in turn and decide which one you most favour:

- divine justice is indeed involved
- the Duke himself is a God-like figure, dispensing justice
- the Duke is blasphemously using 'heaven' to justify his actions
- the Duke is cynically using 'heaven' for his own convenience
- the Duke is deceiving himself, persuading himself he is doing good
- the Duke is lying and exploitative
- Shakespeare wanted to make the audience laugh
- some other interpretation.

2 Prediction

The Duke says he is going to proceed with Angelo 'by cold gradation' (coolly, step by step) and 'well-balanced form' (with due observance to the proper procedures). What images do these phrases conjure up for you? Guess what plans he has in mind.

3 More letters

Write one of the Duke's letters to Angelo (lines 84–90).

4 Ragozine – who was he? (in small groups)

Ragozine is one of those Shakespeare characters who is never seen, but who plays an important part. Invent his history, telling how he ends up in Vienna's prison and showing any connections with the other characters in the play.

---

omit leave for the time being
visage face, head
presently immediately
prefixed fixed in advance
continue keep
holds cells

journal daily
yonder generation the world outside
free dependant willing servant
consecrated fount holy well

PROVOST   Here in the prison, father,   60
There died this morning of a cruel fever
One Ragozine, a most notorious pirate,
A man of Claudio's years, his beard and head
Just of his colour. What if we do omit
This reprobate till he were well inclined,   65
And satisfy the deputy with the visage
Of Ragozine, more like to Claudio?
DUKE Oh, 'tis an accident that heaven provides:
Dispatch it presently, the hour draws on
Prefixed by Angelo. See this be done   70
And sent according to command, whiles I
Persuade this rude wretch willingly to die.
PROVOST This shall be done, good father, presently:
But Barnardine must die this afternoon,
And how shall we continue Claudio,   75
To save me from the danger that might come
If he were known alive?
DUKE   Let this be done:
Put them in secret holds, both Barnardine and Claudio.
Ere twice the sun hath made his journal greeting
To yonder generation you shall find   80
Your safety manifested.
PROVOST I am your free dependant.
DUKE Quick, dispatch, and send the head to Angelo.

Exit [Provost]

Now will I write letters to Angelo,
The provost he shall bear them, whose contents   85
Shall witness to him I am near at home
And that by great injunctions I am bound
To enter publicly. Him I'll desire
To meet me at the consecrated fount
A league below the city; and from thence,   90
By cold gradation and well-balanced form
We shall proceed with Angelo.

Enter PROVOST *[with a head]*

PROVOST Here is the head, I'll carry it myself.
DUKE Convenient is it. Make a swift return,
For I would commune with you of such things   95
That want no ear but yours.
PROVOST   I'll make all speed.   *Exit*

*The Duke tells Isabella that Claudio has been executed. He promises her
that the Duke is about to return, and that she will be able to take her
revenge on Angelo.*

1 Why does the Duke lie to Isabella? (in pairs)

The Duke tells the audience that he is going to let Isabella believe
that Claudio is dead so that her eventual surprise and relief will be all
the greater (lines 100–2). Talk together about this decision of the
Duke's, particularly what you think of his professed motivation.

2 'Every syllable a faithful verity'
(in groups of about seven to ten)

Two members of the group take the parts of the Duke and Isabella,
and they read lines 103–28 out loud. The rest of the group listen
carefully and either hiss or call out whenever they think they can spot
the Duke telling a lie.

Afterwards, talk about what you think of the Duke at this point, and
what you would want to tell Isabella about him.

3 Revenge (in small groups)

Does Isabella's line 111 seem 'in character'? Why or why not?

The Duke (in the guise of a holy man) promises Isabella (a nun)
'revenges to your heart'. Share what you know about Christian
teaching on revenge (for example, Old Testament: 'an eye for an eye';
New Testament: 'forgive your enemies'). Then consider again your
response to Isabella's line 111.

4 'I am directed by you'

How should Isabella say line 128? Give reasons for your suggestions.

---

close silent
verity truth
covent convent, friary

instance news or proof
bosom heart's desire

ISABELLA [*Within*] Peace, ho, be here.
DUKE The tongue of Isabel. She's come to know
      If yet her brother's pardon be come hither:
      But I will keep her ignorant of her good   100
      To make her heavenly comforts of despair
      When it is least expected.

Enter ISABELLA

ISABELLA Ho, by your leave.
DUKE Good morning to you, fair and gracious daughter.
ISABELLA The better given me by so holy a man.   105
      Hath yet the deputy sent my brother's pardon?
DUKE He hath released him, Isabel, from the world:
      His head is off, and sent to Angelo.
ISABELLA Nay, but it is not so!
DUKE   It is no other.
      Show your wisdom, daughter, in your close patience.   110
ISABELLA Oh, I will to him and pluck out his eyes!
DUKE You shall not be admitted to his sight.
ISABELLA Unhappy Claudio, wretched Isabel,
      Injurious world, most damnèd Angelo!
DUKE This nor hurts him nor profits you a jot.   115
      Forbear it therefore, give your cause to heaven.
      Mark what I say, which you shall find
      By every syllable a faithful verity:
      The Duke comes home tomorrow – nay, dry your eyes –
      One of our covent, and his confessor,   120
      Gives me this instance. Already he hath carried
      Notice to Escalus and Angelo,
      Who do prepare to meet him at the gates,
      There to give up their power. If you can pace your wisdom
      In that good path that I would wish it go,   125
      And you shall have your bosom on this wretch,
      Grace of the Duke, revenges to your heart,
      And general honour.
ISABELLA   I am directed by you.

The Duke arranges for Friar Peter to prepare Isabella and Mariana for the next day's public exposure of Angelo. Lucio comforts Isabella. He insinuates to the 'friar' that the Duke was lecherous.

1 Lucio (in pairs)

Lucio makes comments involving two women: Isabella (lines 143–8) and the 'wench' he got pregnant (lines 158–61). Talk together about what you think of Lucio's attitude to women, and what kind of man he seems to be.

2 Tell Kate Keepdown's story!

Tell the story of Lucio's 'wench' (Kate Keepdown) from her point of view and in a way which is sympathetic to her.

3 Continue the dialogue (in pairs)

The scene ends with the Duke and Lucio talking as they accompany each other to the 'lane's end'. What kind of things might Lucio go on to say to the 'friar'? Improvise another few minutes of dialogue between the two characters. Remember that Lucio has promised to tell 'pretty tales of the Duke'.

4 Another letter, another off-stage meeting

Write the Duke's letter to Friar Peter, and the Duke's notes for his discussion with Peter that evening.

5 'The old fantastical Duke of dark corners'

You have been asked to design a cover for a new edition of the play. The publisher asks you for a picture to illustrate Lucio's description of the Duke (lines 146–7). Draw or paint it.

---

perfect fully inform
home and home totally, right to the heart
combinèd constrained
fain obliged

set me to't sexually arouse me
beholding indebted
woodman womaniser
medlar prostitute

DUKE This letter then to Friar Peter give,
      'Tis that he sent me of the Duke's return.   130
      Say by this token I desire his company
      At Mariana's house tonight. Her cause and yours
      I'll perfect him withal, and he shall bring you
      Before the Duke; and to the head of Angelo
      Accuse him home and home. For my poor self,   135
      I am combinèd by a sacred vow
      And shall be absent. Wend you with this letter:
      Command these fretting waters from your eyes
      With a light heart; trust not my holy order
      If I pervert your course. Who's here?   140

Enter LUCIO

LUCIO Good even; friar, where's the provost?
DUKE Not within, sir.
LUCIO Oh pretty Isabella, I am pale at mine heart to see thine eyes so
      red: thou must be patient. I am fain to dine and sup with water
      and bran; I dare not for my head fill my belly, one fruitful meal   145
      would set me to't. But they say the Duke will be here tomorrow.
      By my troth, Isabel, I loved thy brother; if the old fantastical
      Duke of dark corners had been at home, he had lived.
                                            [Exit Isabella]
DUKE Sir, the Duke is marvellous little beholding to your reports,
      but the best is, he lives not in them.   150
LUCIO Friar, thou knowest not the Duke so well as I do: he's a better
      woodman than thou tak'st him for.
DUKE Well; you'll answer this one day. Fare ye well.
LUCIO Nay, tarry, I'll go along with thee. I can tell thee pretty tales of
      the Duke.   155
DUKE You have told me too many of him already, sir, if they be true;
      if not true, none were enough.
LUCIO I was once before him for getting a wench with child.
DUKE Did you such a thing?
LUCIO Yes, marry, did I; but I was fain to forswear it, they would else   160
      have married me to the rotten medlar.
DUKE Sir, your company is fairer than honest, rest you well.
LUCIO By my troth, I'll go with thee to the lane's end. If bawdy talk
      offend you, we'll have very little of it. Nay, friar, I am a kind of
      burr, I shall stick.   *Exeunt* 165

Angelo and Escalus are puzzled by the contradictory letters from the Duke.
They have instructions to meet the Duke at the city gates. Alone,
Angelo reveals his anxiety about his rape of Isabella.

1 Angelo's soliloquy (in groups of about ten)

Carefully read lines 18–32 and summarise what you think Angelo is saying. Many of the words used carry sexual meaning: 'deed', 'unshapes', 'unpregnant', 'deflowered', 'body', 'enforced', 'tender shame', 'maiden loss' (loss of virginity), 'credent bulk' (large physical size, giving credibility), 'touch', 'dangerous sense' (sensuality).

Divide the speech up between the members of your group. Each person learns their given line or sense unit by repeating it aloud several times in different styles. For example:

- get together in pairs and say the words as if you are lovers
- whisper the words breathlessly to each other
- stand in a circle, all facing the same direction, and one by one pass your line on to the person in front of you
- say them to each other sleepily, angrily, conspiratorially.

When you all know your lines, repeat the soliloquy in its correct order. Now experiment with ways of making a group presentation of the speech, using movement and tone of voice to create what seems to you to be an appropriate mood. You could add music as accompaniment. Compare your dramatisations with those of other groups.

---

disvouched contradicted
dispatch prompt settlement
devices false charges
betimes early
sort and suit rank, importance

unpregnant slow-witted
tongue denounce
dares her no frightens her into
saying nothing

ACT 4   SCENE 4
A room in Angelo's house

Enter ANGELO and ESCALUS

ESCALUS Every letter he hath writ hath disvouched other.

ANGELO In most uneven and distracted manner. His actions show
much like to madness; pray heaven his wisdom be not tainted.
And why meet him at the gates, and redeliver our authorities
there?   5

ESCALUS I guess not.

ANGELO And why should we proclaim it in an hour before his
entering, that if any crave redress of injustice they should exhibit
their petitions in the street?

ESCALUS He shows his reason for that: to have a dispatch of   10
complaints, and to deliver us from devices hereafter, which shall
then have no power to stand against us.

ANGELO Well; I beseech you let it be proclaimed betimes i'th'morn.
I'll call you at your house. Give notice to such men of sort and
suit as are to meet him.   15

ESCALUS I shall, sir. Fare you well.

ANGELO Good night.

Exit [Escalus]

This deed unshapes me quite, makes me unpregnant
And dull to all proceedings. A deflowered maid,
And by an eminent body that enforced   20
The law against it? But that her tender shame
Will not proclaim against her maiden loss,
How might she tongue me? Yet reason dares her no;

Angelo hopes his high office will protect him from scandal, but he expresses his repressed guilt for the death of Claudio and for raping Isabella. In Scene 5 the Duke arranges his return to Vienna.

1 Covering up: an improvisation (in groups of five)

Improvise a short play about someone misusing their authority in order to avoid scandal. Can you think of recent real-life incidents from the news?

2 Angelo's state of mind

Angelo seems to be revealing some of his innermost thoughts to the audience between lines 18 and 32. Imagine that he was in the habit of writing a diary. What do you think would be his diary entry for this particular day? Write it, taking care to bring out the conflicting emotions he seems to be revealing in his soliloquy and his feelings on anticipating the Duke's return the next day.

3 Claudio: revenge or forgiveness?

Do you share Angelo's view of Claudio's character in lines 26–30? Talk together about whether you think Claudio would kill or forgive Angelo.

4 More letters (in pairs)

In Scene 5, yet more letters are mentioned by the Duke. Can you recollect what other letters have so far changed hands throughout the play? Design a diagram which shows what use Shakespeare makes of the letters device in the play.

5 Who's who?

Invent short biographies for Flavius, Valencius, Rowland, Crassus and Varrius. Make your biographies relevant to Angelo's Vienna.

credent bulk huge credibility
tane taken
fit fitting

afoot under way
drift intention, plan
blench deviate

For my authority bears of a credent bulk,
That no particular scandal once can touch   25
But it confounds the breather. He should have lived,
Save that his riotous youth with dangerous sense
Might in the times to come have tane revenge
By so receiving a dishonoured life
With ransom of such shame. Would yet he had lived.   30
Alack, when once our grace we have forgot,
Nothing goes right: we would, and we would not.   *Exit*

ACT 4   SCENE 5
Vienna   A monastery

Enter DUKE *in his own robes and* FRIAR PETER

DUKE These letters at fit time deliver me.
         The provost knows our purpose and our plot.
         The matter being afoot, keep your instruction
         And hold you ever to our special drift,
         Though sometimes you do blench from this to that   5
         As cause doth minister. Go call at Flavius' house,
         And tell him where I stay; give the like notice
         To Valencius, Rowland, and to Crassus,
         And bid them bring the trumpets to the gate.
         But send me Flavius first.
FRIAR PETER   It shall be speeded well.   [*Exit*]   10

Enter VARRIUS

DUKE I thank thee, Varrius, thou hast made good haste.
         Come, we will walk, there's other of our friends
         Will greet us here anon, my gentle Varrius.
                                                         Exeunt

Isabella instructs Mariana to follow the 'friar's' plan. Isabella will accuse Angelo of rape, but Mariana will reveal the truth. Friar Peter urges the two women to the city gates.

1 Telling a friend (in pairs)

It is the morning after Mariana has slept with Angelo. The whole rendezvous has taken place off-stage, for obvious reasons. But what would Mariana have said about it all to Isabella? She's probably not going to be too explicit about the details, since she is talking to a nun, but the two women are likely to be close enough to confide their feelings to one another. Improvise their conversation.

2 The scene is set (in groups of five or six)

Friar Peter's lines 10–15 set the scene for the Duke's grand return to Vienna. They also raise the tension for the dénouement of the play. The Duke's return will be a great state occasion. Today it would be covered by television news.

Imagine that you work for the Vienna Broadcasting Company. You have a special programme slot reporting on the homecoming of the Duke. Your instructions are to include:

- 'vox pop' interviews on the streets gauging public opinion of the Duke
- studio interviews with political commentators and a gossip columnist
- a reporter on the spot describing the scene on the streets as they wait for their first glimpse of their ruler.

Put your television programme together and 'broadcast' it, using the rest of the class as the crowd where necessary.

---

loath reluctant
veil full purpose conceal the full plan
peradventure by chance
physic medicine
to sweet end to ensure a happy outcome

stand place to stand
generous and gravest the most high-born and dignified
hent arrived at

ACT 4 SCENE 6
Vienna A Street

Enter ISABELLA *and* MARIANA

ISABELLA To speak so indirectly I am loath;
       I would say the truth, but to accuse him so
       That is your part, yet I am advised to do it:
       He says, to veil full purpose.
MARIANA   Be ruled by him.
ISABELLA Besides, he tells me that if peradventure   5
       He speak against me on the adverse side
       I should not think it strange, for 'tis a physic
       That's bitter to sweet end.

Enter FRIAR PETER

MARIANA I would Friar Peter –
ISABELLA   Oh peace, the friar is come.
FRIAR PETER Come, I have found you out a stand most fit,   10
       Where you may have such vantage on the Duke
       He shall not pass you. Twice have the trumpets sounded.
       The generous and gravest citizens
       Have hent the gates, and very near upon
       The Duke is ent'ring; therefore hence, away.   15
                                  Exeunt

Looking back at Act 4
Activities for groups or individuals

1 Structure of scenes

On a large sheet of paper copy and complete the diagram below.

Act 4	Place	Which characters involved?	Length of scene	What happens?
Scene 1	Mariana's 'moated grange'	Mariana, Duke, Isabella	73 lines	The Duke and Isabella tell Mariana...
Scene 2	The prison			
Scene 3				
Scene 4				
Scene 5				
Scene 6				

When you have finished the diagram, talk together about the dramatic effect of having a number of short scenes with different settings.

Identify how each of these settings contrasts with the others. Work out how you would suggest each change of scene on stage using music, lighting, background noise, stage furniture or props.

2 Mariana at the moated grange (in pairs)

Consider each of the following 'readings' in turn:

- she is a romantic figure
- she is someone you pity
- she is a fully realised, three-dimensional character
- she has only one function in the play: to provide a way of avoiding Isabella losing her virginity
- Mariana's feelings are important for an audience to experience
- you are never invited to consider Mariana's feelings
- Mariana's trust in the Duke says more about his character than hers.

What 'evidence' could be produced to support each reading?

3 The Duke's actions (in groups of three or four)

In Act 4, the Duke's role clearly changes from the observer of others to an active participant. Compile a list of all the Duke's actions in the act. Make and show a series of tableaux, one for each item on your list, to illustrate the actions the Duke performs.

4 A severed head (in small groups)

In Scene 3, line 92 the Provost enters 'with a head'. This stage direction could be played on stage in a number of different ways, depending on the particular effect you wish to achieve:

a You could play up the humorous possibilities, emphasising that the play is a comedy.

b You could go for gruesome realism. The head would remind your audience that a man has actually been executed under the corrupt penal system of Vienna. The grim reality of such a death faces some of the main characters.

If you were directing the play, how would you present this moment? Try acting the scene out in a variety of ways. Give thought to the nature of the 'prop' you would use.

Criminals were often 'hanged, drawn and quartered'.

The Duke is greeted by Angelo and Escalus. He publicly praises Angelo.
Isabella cries out for justice.

---

1 Dramatic irony (in groups of three)

The Duke's language in Act 5 is rich in dramatic irony. His words carry a deeper meaning for the audience than is perceived by Angelo.

One person reads the Duke's lines 1–18, pausing at each punctuation mark. At each pause, a second person, as Angelo, interprets the remark. The third person states the Duke's hidden meaning, for example:

Person 1 (The Duke): 'My very worthy cousin'
Person 2 (Angelo): 'He thinks highly of me, like a close relative.'
Person 3 (the Duke's secret thoughts): 'Worthy – of little worth!'

2 Angelo's deserving

Lines 9–13 embody one of Shakespeare's favourite images: how time destroys love, life and reputation.

'envious calumniating time' (*Troilus and Cressida*)
'cormorant devouring time' (*Love's Labour's Lost*)
'Mis-shapen time . . . eater of youth' (*The Rape of Lucrece*)
'Time's scythe' (Sonnet 12)
'Devouring time' (Sonnet 19)

Shakespeare was also fascinated by brass inscriptions (as in church memorials) which try to preserve, against the despoiling erasures of time, the reputations of great men (Sonnet 64 has several echoes of lines 11–13).

- Make a drawing to illustrate 'the tooth of time' (line 12).
- Design a brass memorial to Angelo.

3 'Justice, justice, justice, justice!'

Advise Isabella how each 'justice' (line 25) should be spoken.

---

forerunning more requital ahead
  of further reward
bonds obligation to you
desert deserving
To lock . . . bosom to hide it away

forted strong
razure erasure
subject citizens
fain gladly
vail your regard look down

ACT 5   SCENE 1
Vienna   The City Gate

Enter DUKE *in his own robes,* VARRIUS, LORDS, ANGELO, ESCALUS,
LUCIO, PROVOST, OFFICERS, CITIZENS, *at several doors*

DUKE My very worthy cousin, fairly met.
        Our old and faithful friend, we are glad to see you.
ANGELO *and* ESCALUS Happy return be to your royal grace.
DUKE Many and hearty thankings to you both:
        We have made enquiry of you, and we hear   5
        Such goodness of your justice that our soul
        Cannot but yield you forth to public thanks
        Forerunning more requital.
ANGELO   You make my bonds still greater.
DUKE Oh, your desert speaks loud, and I should wrong it
        To lock it in the wards of covert bosom   10
        When it deserves with characters of brass
        A forted residence 'gainst the tooth of time
        And razure of oblivion. Give me your hand
        And let the subject see, to make them know
        That outward courtesies would fain proclaim   15
        Favours that keep within. Come, Escalus,
        You must walk by us on our other hand:
        And good supporters are you.

Enter FRIAR PETER *and* ISABELLA

FRIAR PETER Now is your time. Speak loud, and kneel before him.
ISABELLA Justice, oh royal Duke! Vail your regard   20
        Upon a wronged – I would fain have said a maid.
        Oh worthy prince, dishonour not your eye
        By throwing it on any other object
        Till you have heard me in my true complaint
        And given me justice, justice, justice, justice!   25

Isabella begins to catalogue Angelo's offences. The Duke says that she is mad and orders her to be removed. Isabella implores him to believe her charge that the perfect-seeming Angelo is a villain.

1 The force of repetition (in pairs)

Isabella appeals for 'justice, justice, justice, justice!' (line 25). Repeating a word or phrase can give great power to argument. Shakespeare strengthens Isabella's pleading to the Duke by different forms of repetition.

Choose one or more of the following to explore how Isabella gives extra emphasis to her entreaties for justice.

a Echoing
One person reads; the other echoes and emphasises the repeated word:

lines 30–2   'hear'
lines 36–42   'strange'
lines 43–6   'true'

Isabella also repeats another simple word to great effect. What is it?

b Listening and repeating
Isabella picks up and repeats words, phrases or ideas from what the Duke or Angelo says to her or about her. Identify how she does this in each of her five speeches opposite.

c Lists
Isabella offers three lists which describe Angelo's reality or appearance in different ways. Find ways to represent one or more of Isabella's 'listings' of Angelo:

lines 38–42   (five items)
line 54   (four items)
lines 55–56   (four items – or eight?).

---

forsworn perjured, a liar upon oath
to th'end of reck'ning to the end
  of time
conjure entreat, appeal to
caitiff villain

absolute perfect
dressings robes
characts insignia of office
forms ceremonies

DUKE   Relate your wrongs: in what? By whom? Be brief.
        Here is Lord Angelo shall give you justice;
        Reveal yourself to him.
ISABELLA   Oh worthy Duke,
        You bid me seek redemption of the devil.
        Hear me yourself: for that which I must speak   30
        Must either punish me, not being believed,
        Or wring redress from you. Hear me, oh hear me, here!
ANGELO   My lord, her wits I fear me are not firm;
        She hath been a suitor to me for her brother
        Cut off by course of justice.
ISABELLA   By course of justice!   35
ANGELO   And she will speak most bitterly and strange.
ISABELLA   Most strange, but yet most truly will I speak.
        That Angelo's forsworn, is it not strange?
        That Angelo's a murderer, is't not strange?
        That Angelo is an adulterous thief,   40
        An hypocrite, a virgin-violator,
        Is it not strange, and strange?
DUKE   Nay, it is ten times strange.
ISABELLA   It is not truer he is Angelo
        Than this is all as true as it is strange;
        Nay, it is ten times true, for truth is truth   45
        To th'end of reck'ning.
DUKE   Away with her: poor soul,
        She speaks this in th'infirmity of sense.
ISABELLA   Oh prince, I conjure thee as thou believ'st
        There is another comfort than this world,
        That thou neglect me not with that opinion   50
        That I am touched with madness: make not impossible
        That which but seems unlike. 'Tis not impossible
        But one, the wicked'st caitiff on the ground,
        May seem as shy, as grave, as just, as absolute
        As Angelo; even so may Angelo   55
        In all his dressings, characts, titles, forms,
        Be an arch-villain. Believe it, royal prince,
        If he be less, he's nothing, but he's more,
        Had I more name for badness.

Isabella begins to tell her story to the Duke. Lucio supports her, but his interjections are rebuked by the Duke.

Who's who? Identify the characters in this 1940 Shakespeare Memorial Theatre production. What line do you think is being spoken at this moment?

1 Lucio's interruptions (in groups of three)

Take parts and read lines 69–87 in a variety of ways. As you do so, talk together about some of the following:

- Is the Duke angered or amused by Lucio (or some other reaction)?
- How does Isabella react to Lucio's 'help'?
- What tone do you think is most appropriate for Lucio to use?

  Experiment with different styles:

  genuinely trying to be helpful
  a busybody
  fearful, but wanting to speak
  knowing the Duke has been disguised as a friar.

---

frame of sense logical structure
inequality injustice (or unequal
  status). No one can be quite sure
  which meaning is intended. Which
  do you prefer?

an't and it (if it)
pernicious caitiff malevolent
  villain

DUKE   By mine honesty,
　　If she be mad – as I believe no other –   60
　　Her madness hath the oddest frame of sense,
　　Such a dependency of thing on thing,
　　As e'er I heard in madness.
ISABELLA   Oh, gracious Duke,
　　Harp not on that; nor do not banish reason
　　For inequality, but let your reason serve   65
　　To make the truth appear where it seems hid,
　　And hide the false seems true.
DUKE   Many that are not mad
　　Have sure more lack of reason. What would you say?
ISABELLA I am the sister of one Claudio,
　　Condemned upon the act of fornication   70
　　To lose his head, condemned by Angelo.
　　I, in probation of a sisterhood,
　　Was sent to by my brother; one Lucio
　　As then the messenger –
LUCIO   That's I, an't like your grace.
　　I came to her from Claudio, and desired her   75
　　To try her gracious fortune with Lord Angelo
　　For her poor brother's pardon.
ISABELLA   That's he indeed.
DUKE [*To Lucio*] You were not bid to speak.
LUCIO   No, my good lord,
　　Nor wished to hold my peace.
DUKE   I wish you now then.
　　Pray you take note of it; and when you have   80
　　A business for yourself, pray heaven you then
　　Be perfect.
LUCIO   I warrant your honour.
DUKE The warrant's for yourself: take heed to't.
ISABELLA This gentleman told somewhat of my tale.
LUCIO Right.   85
DUKE It may be right, but you are i'th'wrong
　　To speak before your time. Proceed.
ISABELLA   I went
　　To this pernicious caitiff deputy –
DUKE That's somewhat madly spoken.
ISABELLA   Pardon it,
　　The phrase is to the matter.   90

Isabella tells of Angelo's broken bargain: her chastity for Claudio's life. The Duke refuses to believe her, praising Angelo's integrity. He commits Isabella to prison.

1 A difficult story (in pairs or groups of three)

Isabella, a novice nun, has a difficult tale to tell. Not only must she speak openly about sex, but she must also tell a downright lie ('And I did yield to him'). Find a way of representing her story, showing as many as possible of the actions and feelings described in lines 92–103. It could be:

- as a mime to the narrated story
- as a series of cartoons, with captions
- as a graph or diagram, plotting the movement of Isabella's feelings
- as keywords: for example, using only nouns, verbs and adjectives in a staccato rendering. Don't worry if it takes you a little time to get the hang of 'concupiscible'. Everybody has problems at first – but it's a word to relish!

2 Angelo's feelings (in groups of three)

Angelo has been silent since line 35, when he said 'And she will speak most bitterly and strange'. But he must be following intensely all that is said, wondering whether or not he is safe from discovery.

Take parts (Duke, Isabella, Angelo) and work out what Angelo is thinking as he listens to each of the speeches opposite. The Duke and Isabella read aloud, pausing at the end of each sentence. In each pause Angelo states his thoughts and feelings, reporting how secure he feels.

3 Measure for measure

'He would have weighed thy brother by himself'

Make a drawing to illustrate line 111.

---

to set . . . by to cut a long story short	**fond** foolish
refelled rejected, refused	**suborned** bribed
vild vile	**ministers** angels
concupiscible violent sexual appetite	**wrapped up in countenance** hidden by authority
confutes proves false, overcomes	**fain** gladly
	ghostly spiritual (or invisible)

DUKE Mended again: the matter: proceed.
ISABELLA In brief, to set the needless process by.
      How I persuaded, how I prayed, and kneeled,
      How he refelled me, and how I replied –
      For this was of much length – the vild conclusion   95
      I now begin with grief and shame to utter.
      He would not but by gift of my chaste body
      To his concupiscible intemperate lust,
      Release my brother; and after much debatement
      My sisterly remorse confutes mine honour   100
      And I did yield to him. But the next morn betimes,
      His purpose surfeiting, he sends a warrant
      For my poor brother's head.
DUKE   This is most likely!
ISABELLA Oh, that it were as like as it is true.
DUKE By heaven, fond wretch, thou know'st not what thou speak'st,   105
      Or else thou art suborned against his honour
      In hateful practice. First, his integrity
      Stands without blemish; next, it imports no reason
      That with such vehemency he should pursue
      Faults proper to himself. If he had so offended,   110
      He would have weighed thy brother by himself
      And not have cut him off. Some one hath set you on:
      Confess the truth and say by whose advice
      Thou cam'st here to complain.
ISABELLA   And is this all?
      Then, oh you blessèd ministers above,   115
      Keep me in patience, and with ripened time
      Unfold the evil which is here wrapped up
      In countenance. Heaven shield your grace from woe,
      As I, thus wronged, hence unbelievèd go.
DUKE I know you'ld fain be gone. An officer!   120
      To prison with her! Shall we thus permit
      A blasting and a scandalous breath to fall
      On him so near us? This needs must be a practice.
      Who knew of your intent and coming hither?
ISABELLA One that I would were here, Friar Lodowick.   125
DUKE A ghostly father, belike. Who knows that Lodowick?

Lucio maligns Friar Lodowick. Friar Peter asserts that Isabella has wrongly accused Angelo. Peter praises Lodowick, saying that he will support Angelo. Isabella is led off by guards.

---

1 Character reference (in groups of three)

Collect all the descriptions of Friar Lodowick on the opposite page. Arrange them in lists according to whether you think they are true or false.

Take parts as the Duke, Lucio and Friar Peter. Read the opposite page aloud, but every time the Duke is mentioned in any way (as Lodowick or as himself), point to the Duke and say 'That's you!' (the Duke says 'That's me!'). Afterwards, talk together about how this activity adds to your understanding of the Duke's personality, his deceptions, and his official power.

Note: In the first two lines (lines 127–8) there are six such 'pointing' occasions.

2 Surprise?

Friar Peter twice accuses Isabella of lying.

- Why does Peter make the accusations?
- How do both Isabella and Angelo react? Work out what each would do at particular points in Peter's story.

3 Exit Isabella (in pairs)

Talk together about why Isabella is taken off at line 162, rather than at line 125 after the Duke orders her to prison. Discuss whether you think it would be more dramatically effective if Isabella were kept on stage to hear what follows.

---

lay secular, non-religious
swinged thrashed
touch or soil sexual contamination
one ungot a man not born
temporary secular

vouches asserts
mere personal
probation proof
convented sent for
vulgarly publicly

LUCIO My lord, I know him, 'tis a meddling friar.
    I do not like the man: had he been lay, my lord,
    For certain words he spake against your grace
    In your retirement, I had swinged him soundly.   130
DUKE Words against me? This' a good friar, belike;
    And to set on this wretched woman here
    Against our substitute! Let this friar be found.
LUCIO But yesternight, my lord, she and that friar,
    I saw them at the prison: a saucy friar,   135
    A very scurvy fellow.
FRIAR PETER Blessèd be your royal grace.
    I have stood by, my lord, and I have heard
    Your royal ear abused. First hath this woman
    Most wrongfully accused your substitute,   140
    Who is as free from touch or soil with her
    As she from one ungot.
DUKE   We did believe no less.
    Know you that Friar Lodowick that she speaks of?
FRIAR PETER I know him for a man divine and holy,
    Not scurvy, nor a temporary meddler,   145
    As he's reported by this gentleman;
    And on my trust, a man that never yet
    Did, as he vouches, misreport your grace.
LUCIO My lord, most villainously, believe it.
FRIAR PETER Well; he in time may come to clear himself;   150
    But at this instant he is sick, my lord,
    Of a strange fever. Upon his mere request
    Being come to knowledge, that there was complaint
    Intended 'gainst Lord Angelo, came I hither
    To speak as from his mouth what he doth know   155
    Is true and false, and what he with his oath
    And all probation will make up full clear
    Whensoever he's convented. First, for this woman,
    To justify this worthy nobleman
    So vulgarly and personally accused,   160
    Her shall you hear disprovèd to her eyes,
    Till she herself confess it.
                        [Exit Isabella, guarded]
DUKE   Good friar, let's hear it.
    Do you not smile at this, Lord Angelo?

*The Duke appoints Angelo to judge his own case. Mariana, her face veiled,
speaks riddlingly of her husband.*

---

1 'Judge of your own cause' (in small groups)

The Duke appoints Angelo to judge his own case. How similar is 'In
this I'll be impartial' to the opening of the play, where the Duke also
hands over responsibility?

Should anyone ever be both judge and jury in their own case? Talk
together about whether someone involved in a 'case' should ever be
the judge of that case. Use examples from your own experience (for
example, who is the 'judge' in school or college? Should a student
ever be the judge of his or her own case?).

Afterwards, discuss why you think the Duke makes Angelo judge of
his own 'cause'.

2 Mariana and Angelo (in groups of four)

Take parts (as Angelo, the Duke, Lucio and Mariana). Read through
from the entrance of Mariana to line 231 on page 153. Then discuss
how you would heighten the dramatic effects of:

- Lucio's interruptions
- Mariana's riddling replies
- Mariana's unveiling on Angelo's command
- Mariana's repetitions in 204–10 ('This is') and 223–31 ('As')
- Angelo's 'confession' in 214–22.

In your discussions, try to consider:

- Did Shakespeare know that 'trial scenes' always work?
- How this part of the play draws on the romance (or fairy-tale)
  tradition of riddling witnesses and dramatic revelations.
- Dramatic irony (where the audience knows something that Angelo
  does not).

---

punk prostitute
known had sexual intercourse with
And changes him . . . time And
  accuses him of the crime at the very
  moment

depose swear
moe more (other men)

Oh, heaven, the vanity of wretched fools.
Give us some seats. Come, cousin Angelo,   165
In this I'll be impartial: be you judge
Of your own cause.

Enter MARIANA [*veiled*]

Is this the witness, friar?
First let her show her face, and after speak.
MARIANA Pardon, my lord, I will not show my face
Until my husband bid me.   170
DUKE What, are you married?
MARIANA No, my lord.
DUKE Are you a maid?
MARIANA No, my lord.
DUKE A widow, then?   175
MARIANA Neither, my lord.
DUKE Why, you are nothing then: neither maid, widow, nor wife?
LUCIO My lord, she may be a punk, for many of them are neither
     maid, widow, nor wife.
DUKE Silence that fellow. I would he had some cause to prattle for 180
     himself.
LUCIO Well, my lord.
MARIANA My lord, I do confess I ne'er was married,
     And I confess besides I am no maid.
     I have known my husband, yet my husband   185
     Knows not that ever he knew me.
LUCIO He was drunk then, my lord, it can be no better.
DUKE For the benefit of silence, would thou wert so too.
LUCIO Well, my lord.
DUKE This is no witness for Lord Angelo.   190
MARIANA Now I come to't, my lord.
     She that accuses him of fornication
     In self-same manner doth accuse my husband,
     And charges him, my lord, with such a time
     When I'll depose I had him in mine arms   195
     With all th'effect of love.
ANGELO Charges she moe than me?
MARIANA   Not that I know.
DUKE No? You say your husband?

Mariana reveals her face to Angelo. She says that he is her husband and has had sexual intercourse with her, thinking her to be Isabella. Angelo speaks disparagingly of her, and denies her charge.

1 Do you believe Angelo? (in pairs)

Angelo claims that his major reason for breaking off his engagement to Mariana was: 'her reputation was disvalued in levity'.

From what you feel you know about Angelo, suggest three or four examples of Mariana's 'levity' that you think he would object to. Compare your examples with those of other groups. Then consider the other reason he gives: money. How important was that in Angelo's decision?

2 Measure for measure

Angelo is revealed to be virtually in the same position as Claudio. He has had sexual intercourse with Mariana, to whom he was pre-contracted. Explore the parallel situations of Angelo/Mariana and Claudio/Juliet.

Take Angelo's lines 214–22. Inter-cut them with what Claudio says at 1.2.126–36 (p. 15). For example, begin by reading short sections of each speech alternately. Then experiment! Don't be afraid to repeat significant phrases or words. Make the most dramatic presentation you can to bring out similarities between Angelo and Claudio. You could also include what Mariana says in her two speeches opposite.

Pick out all the phrases opposite which echo the situation of Claudio and Juliet.

Write the 'vowed contract' between Angelo and Mariana. Write the same document for Claudio and Juliet. Are there differences?

3 Reactions

How is everyone on stage reacting to what they hear?

---

just true
carnally sexually
proportions dowry
came short of composition were insufficient to fulfil the agreed contract

disvalued in levity made valueless by frivolous behaviour

MARIANA Why just, my lord, and that is Angelo,
Who thinks he knows that he ne'er knew my body,   200
But knows, he thinks, that he knows Isabel's.
ANGELO This is a strange abuse – let's see thy face.
MARIANA [*Unveiling*] My husband bids me, now I will unmask.
This is that face, thou cruel Angelo,
Which once thou swor'st was worth the looking on.   205
This is the hand which with a vowed contract
Was fast belocked in thine. This is the body
That took away the match from Isabel
And did supply thee at thy garden-house
In her imagined person.
DUKE   Know you this woman?   210
LUCIO Carnally, she says.
DUKE Sirrah, no more!
LUCIO Enough, my lord.
ANGELO My lord, I must confess I know this woman,
And five years since there was some speech of marriage   215
Betwixt myself and her; which was broke off,
Partly for that her promisèd proportions
Came short of composition, but in chief
For that her reputation was disvalued
In levity. Since which time of five years   220
I never spake with her, saw her, nor heard from her,
Upon my faith and honour.
MARIANA   Noble prince,
As there comes light from heaven, and words from breath,
As there is sense in truth, and truth in virtue,
I am affianced this man's wife, as strongly   225
As words could make up vows. And, my good lord,
But Tuesday night last gone, in's garden-house,
He knew me as a wife. As this is true,
Let me in safety raise me from my knees,
Or else for ever be confixèd here   230
A marble monument.

The Duke sends Friar Peter to fetch Lodowick. He urges Angelo to be severe in punishment, then leaves him and Escalus to judge the case. Lucio claims that Lodowick has insulted the Duke.

Two images often re-appear throughout Shakespeare's plays: the smiling villain and the idea that things are not as they seem.

1 'I did but smile till now' (line 231)

Earlier in the play, Angelo said, 'Ever till now/When men were fond, I smiled, and wondered how' (2.2.190–1). Only a little while ago (line 163) the Duke asked Angelo, 'Do you not smile at this?' Now Angelo again remarks on his smiling. Shakespeare seems to have had a fascination with smiling villains:

> 'One may smile and smile, and be a villain' (*Hamlet*)
> 'There's daggers in men's smiles' (*Macbeth*)
> 'Why, I can smile, and murder whiles I smile' (*King Henry VI Part 3*)
> 'Some that smile have in their hearts, I fear, millions of mischief' (*Julius Caesar*).

Do you see Angelo as a 'smiler'? Choose one of the following:

- Write a poem or short story entitled 'The Smiler with the Knife'.
- Write an essay on Angelo's character. Call it 'Angelo's Smile'.
- Make a list of what is likely to make Angelo smile.

2 'Cucullus non facit monachum'

'The hood does not make the monk' – Lucio quotes a Latin saying. The idea that appearances are deceptive recurs in every Shakespeare play (for example, *Macbeth*: 'Look like the innocent flower, but be the serpent under it'). *Measure for Measure* is rich in examples of the difference between being and seeming (true nature and outward appearance).

Rank every character in the play on a scale measuring from 'greatest seemer' to 'least deceptive'.

---

scope full extent
informal mad
mightier member politically
  powerful person
Compact Together

sealed in approbation proved
  beyond question
chastisement punishment
notable fellow notorious villain

ANGELO   I did but smile till now.
            Now, good my lord, give me the scope of justice,
            My patience here is touched. I do perceive
            These poor informal women are no more
            But instruments of some more mightier member   235
            That sets them on. Let me have way, my lord,
            To find this practice out.
DUKE   Ay, with my heart,
            And punish them to your height of pleasure.
            Thou foolish friar, and thou pernicious woman
            Compact with her that's gone, think'st thou thy oaths,   240
            Though they would swear down each particular saint,
            Were testimonies against his worth and credit
            That's sealed in approbation? You, Lord Escalus,
            Sit with my cousin, lend him your kind pains
            To find out this abuse, whence 'tis derived.   245
            There is another friar that set them on,
            Let him be sent for.
FRIAR PETER Would he were here, my lord, for he indeed
            Hath set the women on to this complaint.
            Your provost knows the place where he abides,   250
            And he may fetch him.
DUKE   Go, do it instantly.
                                              [*Exit Provost*]
            And you, my noble and well-warranted cousin,
            Whom it concerns to hear this matter forth,
            Do with your injuries as seems you best
            In any chastisement. I for a while will leave you;   255
            But stir not you till you have well determined
            Upon these slanderers.
ESCALUS   My lord, we'll do it throughly.
                                              Exit [Duke]
            Signior Lucio, did not you say you knew that Friar Lodowick to
            be a dishonest person?
LUCIO *Cucullus non facit monachum*, honest in nothing but in his   260
            clothes, and one that hath spoke most villainous speeches of the
            Duke.
ESCALUS We shall entreat you to abide here till he come, and
            enforce them against him. We shall find this friar a notable
            fellow.   265

Escalus questions Friar Lodowick (the Duke in disguise) about prompting Mariana and Isabella to accuse Angelo. The Duke tells the women they will receive no justice from Angelo.

1 Unmasking the disguised Duke (in groups of four)

The action from the entry of the disguised Duke to his unmasking moves very quickly. To gain a first impression, take parts as Escalus, Lucio, Angelo and the Duke, and read lines 275–349.

2 Angelo says little (in small groups)

Talk together about why you think Angelo has so little to say in lines 275–349, even though he is supposed to be acting as judge.

3 Lucio's language

'Every time he opens his mouth, it's jokes, lies, sexual innuendo and sneers', said a student about Lucio's language. Examine each time he speaks up to line 349 to decide if that description is true. Then write two or three sentences giving your own view of Lucio's language.

4 Escalus: a sinister meaning?

'I will go darkly to work with her', says Escalus. What do you think he means?

5 Honouring the devil (in small groups)

Let's occasionally honour the devil, says the disguised Duke (lines 288–9).

Talk together about whether you think he is being ironic, and how he should speak the lines.

Find a way of representing the image in lines 288–9.

---

light wanton, lustful
lamb/fox innocent victim/killer
redress justice

retort reject
manifest obviously just

LUCIO As any in Vienna, on my word.

ESCALUS Call that same Isabel here once again, I would speak with
her.

[Exit an Attendant]

Pray you, my lord, give me leave to question, you shall see how
I'll handle her.   270

LUCIO Not better than he, by her own report.

ESCALUS Say you?

LUCIO Marry, sir, I think if you handled her privately she would
sooner confess, perchance publicly she'll be ashamed.

Enter DUKE *[disguised as a friar]*, PROVOST, ISABELLA, *[guarded]*

ESCALUS I will go darkly to work with her.   275

LUCIO That's the way: for women are light at midnight.

ESCALUS Come on, mistress, here's a gentlewoman denies all that
you have said.

LUCIO My lord, here comes the rascal I spoke of, here with the
provost.   280

ESCALUS In very good time: speak not you to him till we call upon
you.

LUCIO Mum.

ESCALUS Come, sir, did you set these women on to slander Lord
Angelo? They have confessed you did.   285

DUKE 'Tis false.

ESCALUS How? Know you where you are?

DUKE Respect to your great place: and let the devil
        Be sometime honoured for his burning throne.
        Where is the Duke? 'Tis he should hear me speak.   290

ESCALUS The Duke's in us, and we will hear you speak;
        Look you speak justly.

DUKE Boldly at least. But oh, poor souls,
        Come you to seek the lamb here of the fox?
        Good night to your redress. Is the Duke gone?   295
        Then is your cause gone too: the Duke's unjust,
        Thus to retort your manifest appeal
        And put your trial in the villain's mouth
        Which here you come to accuse.

LUCIO This is the rascal, this is he I spoke of.   300

Escalus threatens to torture Lodowick for slandering the Duke and inciting Isabella. The 'friar' defies him and speaks of Vienna's corruption. Lucio accuses Lodowick of speaking ill of the Duke.

1 Who's who? (in groups of five)

Sit in a circle as Escalus, Angelo, the Duke, Isabella and Mariana. One person slowly reads Escalus's lines 301–9. Pause every time a person is mentioned in some way (for example, 'thou', 'friar', 'these women', 'this worthy man'). At every pause, everyone points to the character(s) mentioned.

This 'pointing' of pronouns (him, these, you, and so on) is called deixis (pronounced deyesis). It is an excellent way to ensure that you understand who's who. Try it with other speeches.

2 Corruption boiling and bubbling (in groups or pairs)

- Prepare a mime of what the Duke sees as he walks through Vienna.
- Make a drawing to illustrate the Duke's lines 312–15.
- 'Stews' were brothels. Extend and parody the Duke's culinary metaphor by writing a description of Vienna's corruption in the style of the witches' spells in the cauldron scene in *Macbeth*.

3 Escalus – what's he like?

'To th'rack with him!' threatens Escalus; 'Slander to th'state!'. Yet elsewhere he has appeared to be a kindly man. Make a list of alternative 'readings' of Escalus. Indicate the one you favour.

4 Forfeits in a barber's shop

In Shakespeare's time, barbers displayed comical lists of mock forfeits prescribing what would happen if customers misbehaved.

---

unhallowed unholy
suborned bribed
tax charge
touze pull apart
nor here provincial nor subject to the laws of this place

as much in mock as mark more laughed at than obeyed
Baldpate i.e. friars had shaved heads (tonsures)
fleshmonger pimp
close make amends, compromise

ESCALUS Why, thou unreverend and unhallowed friar!
       Is't not enough thou hast suborned these women
       To accuse this worthy man, but in foul mouth
       And in the witness of his proper ear
       To call him villain, and then to glance from him   305
       To th'Duke himself, to tax him with injustice?
       Take him hence; to th'rack with him! We'll touze you
       Joint by joint, but we will know his purpose.
       What? Unjust?
DUKE   Be not so hot: the Duke
       Dare no more stretch this finger of mine than he   310
       Dare rack his own. His subject am I not,
       Nor here provincial: my business in this state
       Made me a looker-on here in Vienna,
       Where I have seen corruption boil and bubble
       Till it o'errun the stew; laws for all faults,   315
       But faults so countenanced that the strong statutes
       Stand like the forfeits in a barber's shop,
       As much in mock as mark.
ESCALUS   Slander to th'state!
       Away with him to prison!
ANGELO What can you vouch against him, Signior Lucio?   320
       Is this the man that you did tell us of?
LUCIO 'Tis he, my lord. Come hither, goodman Baldpate, do you
    know me?
DUKE I remember you, sir, by the sound of your voice. I met you at
    the prison, in the absence of the Duke.   325
LUCIO Oh, did you so? And do you remember what you said of the
    Duke?
DUKE Most notedly, sir.
LUCIO Do you so, sir? And was the Duke a fleshmonger, a fool, and
    a coward, as you then reported him to be?   330
DUKE You must, sir, change persons with me, ere you make that my
    report: you indeed spoke so of him, and much more, much
    worse.
LUCIO Oh thou damnable fellow, did not I pluck thee by the nose for
    thy speeches?   335
DUKE I protest I love the Duke as I love myself.
ANGELO Hark how the villain would close now, after his treasonable
    abuses.

Escalus orders the 'friar', the women and Peter to prison. Lucio unwittingly unmasks the Duke. Angelo begs the death sentence upon himself. The Duke orders the marriage of Angelo and Mariana.

1 Reactions (in groups of eight)

How does everyone respond when Lucio pulls off the 'friar's' hood to reveal the Duke?

Take parts as the Duke, Angelo, Isabella, Mariana, Escalus, Provost, Lucio, Friar Peter. Prepare a tableau to show the moment of discovery when everyone suddenly realises that the 'friar' is the Duke. Each character should register his or her reaction and feelings at that instant.

Show your tableau to the class, staying stock-still for thirty seconds. The class guesses who represents each character. Afterwards, discuss which character is most easy to identify, and why.

2 Angelo's confession (in pairs)

Speak Angelo's lines 359–67, but punctuate them with extracts from what he said in 2.1.17–31. Bring out how he forecasts his own fate.

Talk together about what Angelo's appeal for instant death adds to your view of his personality and role.

3 The Duke takes charge (in pairs)

As soon as his identity is revealed, the Duke begins to give orders and dispense 'justice'. The language of authority is laden with commands. Read aloud all the Duke says opposite from line 349. How many commands can you find? How many judgements?

---

bolts fetters
giglets prostitutes
knave's visage villainous face
sheep-biting . . . hanged dogs
  that worried sheep were hanged

undiscernible undetectable
passes transgressions, sins
consummate done

ESCALUS Such a fellow is not to be talked withal: away with him to prison. Where is the provost? Away with him to prison. Lay bolts 340
enough upon him. Let him speak no more. Away with those giglets too, and with the other confederate companion.
[The Provost lays hands on the Duke]

DUKE Stay, sir, stay a while.

ANGELO What, resists he? Help him, Lucio!

LUCIO Come, sir, come, sir, come, sir! Foh, sir! Why, you bald- 345
pated, lying rascal, you must be hooded, must you? Show your knave's visage, with a pox to you! Show your sheep-biting face, and be hanged an hour! Will't not off?
[He pulls off the Friar's hood and discovers the Duke]

DUKE Thou art the first knave that e'er mad'st a duke!
First, provost, let me bail these gentle three – 350
[To Lucio] Sneak not away, sir, for the friar and you
Must have a word anon. – Lay hold on him.

LUCIO This may prove worse than hanging.

DUKE *[To Escalus]* What you have spoke, I pardon. Sit you down.
We'll borrow place of him. *[To Angelo]* Sir, by your leave: 355
Hast thou or word or wit or impudence
That yet can do thee office? If thou hast,
Rely upon it till my tale be heard,
And hold no longer out.

ANGELO   Oh, my dread lord,
I should be guiltier than my guiltiness 360
To think I can be undiscernible
When I perceive your grace, like power divine,
Hath looked upon my passes. Then, good prince,
No longer session hold upon my shame,
But let my trial be mine own confession: 365
Immediate sentence then, and sequent death,
Is all the grace I beg.

DUKE   Come hither, Mariana. –
Say, wast thou e'er contracted to this woman?

ANGELO I was, my lord.

DUKE Go, take her hence and marry her instantly. 370
Do you the office, friar, which consummate,
Return him here again. Go with him, provost.
Exeunt [Angelo, Mariana, Friar Peter, Provost]

The Duke reinforces Isabella's belief that Claudio is dead. Upon Angelo's return, the Duke insists on measure for measure: Angelo's life for Claudio's.

1 But why? (in small groups)

Discuss together your views on the following puzzles:

- Why does the Duke keep Isabella ignorant that Claudio lives?
- Why is Isabella's language so humble and unquestioning (unlike her exchanges with Angelo in Act 2)?
- Why does the Duke, while offering mercy to others, continue to condemn Angelo to death?

2 Measure for measure

In lines 402–4 the balance that characterises the whole play, weighing one thing against another, comes to full fruition. Learn the lines. Explore ways of bringing out the balanced words.

- Imagine that you have a bucket in each hand. Walk slowly around the room, speaking the words. Imagine 'placing' each balanced word in one or other bucket as you walk. Feel the weight of the words!
- Link hands with a partner and push and pull on each balanced word.
- Imagine your hands as a pair of scales. 'Weigh' your way through the lines, balancing one word against another.
- Make drawings of each of the six balanced phrases.
- Read St Matthew 7:1–2, Genesis 9:6 and Leviticus 24:17–20. Compare these biblical passages with the Duke's words.
- But is it justice? The Duke is insisting on the moral principle of an eye for an eye and a tooth for a tooth. Talk together about your own views on enforcing that principle
  a   in Angelo's case
  b   in your school or college.

Advertising attentive
Attorneyed acting as agent
vassal subject, servant
rash remonstrance hasty demonstration

celerity speed
brained destroyed (knocked on the head)
salt lustful

ESCALUS My lord, I am more amazed at his dishonour,
　　　　 Than at the strangeness of it.
DUKE   Come hither, Isabel.
　　　　 Your friar is now your prince: as I was then,   375
　　　　 Advertising and holy to your business,
　　　　 Not changing heart with habit, I am still
　　　　 Attorneyed at your service.
ISABELLA   Oh, give me pardon
　　　　 That I, your vassal, have employed and pained
　　　　 Your unknown sovereignty.
DUKE   You are pardoned, Isabel: 380
　　　　 And now dear maid, be you as free to us.
　　　　 Your brother's death I know sits at your heart,
　　　　 And you may marvel why I obscured myself,
　　　　 Labouring to save his life, and would not rather
　　　　 Make rash remonstrance of my hidden power   385
　　　　 Than let him so be lost. Oh, most kind maid,
　　　　 It was the swift celerity of his death
　　　　 Which I did think with slower foot came on
　　　　 That brained my purpose – but peace be with him.
　　　　 That life is better life, past fearing death,   390
　　　　 Than that which lives to fear: make it your comfort,
　　　　 So happy is your brother.
ISABELLA   I do, my lord.

Enter ANGELO, MARIANA, FRIAR PETER [*and*] PROVOST

DUKE For this new-married man approaching here,
　　　　 Whose salt imagination yet hath wronged
　　　　 Your well-defended honour, you must pardon   395
　　　　 For Mariana's sake. But as he adjudged your brother,
　　　　 Being criminal in double violation
　　　　 Of sacred chastity and of promise-breach
　　　　 Thereon dependent for your brother's life,
　　　　 The very mercy of the law cries out   400
　　　　 Most audible, even from his proper tongue:
　　　　 An Angelo for Claudio, death for death;
　　　　 Haste still pays haste, and leisure answers leisure;
　　　　 Like doth quit like, and measure still for measure.

Angelo is condemned to death by beheading. Mariana begs for her husband's life. She implores Isabella to join her in pleading to the Duke for mercy towards Angelo.

1 Characters under stress (in small groups)

The Duke puts both women under great stress. He tells Mariana that the husband she has just married must be executed. When Mariana appeals to Isabella to support her plea for Angelo's life, the Duke reminds Isabella of the dead Claudio. To ask for mercy for the man who has murdered her brother is against all reason and affection. Her brother's ghost would return to haunt her.

Mariana's appeal puts more pressure on Isabella. Why should she beg forgiveness for, not vengeance on, the man who wished to rape her and who, she thinks, has killed her brother? Now Mariana asks her 'Will you not lend a knee?' What should she do?

- Revenge or mercy? Take sides and argue for and against whether Isabella should help Mariana by pleading for Angelo's life.

- Inside Isabella's mind. In the 1950 Stratford production, there was an extremely long pause after the Duke's line 436. The director, Peter Brook, told Barbara Jefford, playing Isabella, to remain silent for as long as she could before replying. Talk together about all the thoughts that go through Isabella's mind in that long pause.

- Inside the Duke's mind. Why does he put so much pressure on Isabella? Talk through the reasons he has in his mind when he says 'He dies for Claudio's death'.

- Improvise. Make up a similar example where you are being asked to plead for mercy for a person who has done you great wrong. Talk together about what you would do, and why.

2 Angelo's silence

Angelo is silent after the Duke's death sentence. If Shakespeare had written Angelo's reply after line 408, what would he say?

---

manifested made clear
denies thee vantage you'll get no pardon
imputation . . . you gossip that he had had sex with you

choke your good to come spoil your future prospects
we are definitive my decision will never change
importune request
pavèd bed gravestone

Then, Angelo, thy fault's thus manifested   405
Which, though thou wouldst deny, denies thee vantage.
We do condemn thee to the very block
Where Claudio stooped to death, and with like haste.
Away with him.

MARIANA   Oh, my most gracious lord,
I hope you will not mock me with a husband?   410
DUKE It is your husband mocked you with a husband;
Consenting to the safeguard of your honour,
I thought your marriage fit: else imputation,
For that he knew you, might reproach your life
And choke your good to come. For his possessions,   415
Although by confiscation they are ours,
We do instate and widow you with all
To buy you a better husband.
MARIANA   Oh, my dear lord,
I crave no other, nor no better man.
DUKE Never crave him, we are definitive.   420
MARIANA Gentle my liege – [*Kneeling*]
DUKE   You do but lose your labour.
Away with him to death. [*To Lucio*] Now, sir, to you.
MARIANA Oh my good lord! Sweet Isabel, take my part,
Lend me your knees, and all my life to come
I'll lend you all my life to do you service.   425
DUKE Against all sense you do importune her.
Should she kneel down in mercy of this fact,
Her brother's ghost his pavèd bed would break
And take her hence in horror.
MARIANA   Isabel!
Sweet Isabel, do yet but kneel by me,   430
Hold up your hands, say nothing; I'll speak all.
They say best men are moulded out of faults,
And for the most become much more the better
For being a little bad: so may my husband.
Oh Isabel! Will you not lend a knee?   435
DUKE He dies for Claudio's death.

Isabella kneels and pleads for Angelo's life, saying he only intended, but did not commit, a sexual crime. The Duke dismisses the Provost and sends for Barnardine. Angelo expresses repentance and begs for death.

1 Isabella's plea

Speak lines 436–47 in different ways to each other: passionately, hesitantly, coldly and formally, and so on. Which tone is most appropriate?

Isabella gives three main reasons to support her plea that Angelo should be pardoned: (a) Judge Angelo as if Claudio lived; (b) Angelo was good until he saw me; (c) Claudio did the deed, Angelo only thought it. Identify the actual sentences in which she gives each reason, and read each in turn. Discuss the strengths and weaknesses of each reason.

Do you think Isabella really believes each of the reasons she offers, or is she more motivated by sympathy for Mariana – or some other emotion?

2 Is Isabella vain? A man's view

'I partly think/A due sincerity governed his deeds/Till he did look on me'. Dr Samuel Johnson, a famous eighteenth-century Shakespeare critic, thought that these lines meant that Shakespeare intended 'that women think ill of nothing that raises the credit of their beauty, and are ready, however virtuous, to pardon any act which they think is incited by their own charms'.

Talk together about whether you think that is true of Isabella (and of women generally). Or is it just a false, common belief held by men?

3 Is Angelo sincere?

Lines 467–70 are Angelo's final words in the play. He expresses contrition for his deeds. Explore different ways of speaking them, to find whether you feel they are sincerely intended.

---

no subjects not subject to the law (or, not like a king's subjects)
suit's pleading is
advice thought

still always
procure cause
penitent repentant

ISABELLA [*Kneeling*]   Most bounteous sir,
     Look if it please you on this man condemned
     As if my brother lived. I partly think
     A due sincerity governed his deeds
     Till he did look on me. Since it is so,   440
     Let him not die. My brother had but justice,
     In that he did the thing for which he died.
     For Angelo,
     His act did not o'ertake his bad intent,
     And must be buried but as an intent   445
     That perished by the way. Thoughts are no subjects,
     Intents but merely thoughts.
MARIANA   Merely, my lord.
DUKE Your suit's unprofitable. Stand up, I say.
     I have bethought me of another fault:
     Provost, how came it Claudio was beheaded   450
     At an unusual hour?
PROVOST   It was commanded so.
DUKE Had you a special warrant for the deed?
PROVOST No, my good lord: it was by private message.
DUKE For which I do discharge you of your office;
     Give up your keys.
PROVOST   Pardon me, noble lord,   455
     I thought it was a fault, but knew it not,
     Yet did repent me after more advice;
     For testimony whereof, one in the prison
     That should by private order else have died
     I have reserved alive.
DUKE   What's he?
PROVOST   His name is Barnardine.   460
DUKE I would thou hadst done so by Claudio.
     Go fetch him hither. Let me look upon him.
                         [*Exit Provost*]
ESCALUS I am sorry one so learned and so wise
     As you, Lord Angelo, have still appeared,
     Should slip so grossly, both in the heat of blood   465
     And lack of tempered judgement afterward.
ANGELO I am sorry that such sorrow I procure,
     And so deep sticks it in my penitent heart
     That I crave death more willingly than mercy.
     'Tis my deserving, and I do entreat it.   470

> *The Duke pardons Barnardine. Claudio is revealed alive and is also pardoned, as is Angelo. The Duke proposes marriage to Isabella. Lucio is sentenced to marry a prostitute and be whipped and hanged.*

1 Isabella's silence

Many people find it strange that Isabella says nothing to her brother, or about the Duke's proposal in line 485.

Write two short speeches for her, of four lines each: one to Claudio after he is revealed; the other to the Duke's proposal.

2 Other silences

Other characters are silent as the Duke dispenses the 'justice' that will so intensely affect their future lives. Work out what one of the following characters would say and do in response to the Duke's 'justice': Claudio (on seeing Isabella and Juliet, and hearing the Duke's pardon); or Barnardine (on his pardon); or Angelo (on his pardon); or Mariana (on Angelo's pardon); or Juliet (has she had her baby?) on Claudio's pardon.

3 But why?

Why do you think Shakespeare keeps all these characters silent? Draw up a list offering as many reasons as possible.

4 Changing tones of voice (in pairs)

One person suggests the tone of voice suitable for each section of all the Duke says opposite. The other person speaks each section in the suggested manner.

5 More pressure: moral blackmail?

The Duke takes advantage of Claudio's being discovered alive to propose marriage to Isabella. Are lines 483–6 moral blackmail?

---

muffled blindfolded or hooded
squar'st regulates, lives out
quit pardon, acquit
her worth, worth yours she and you are of equal value and status

apt remission willing forgiveness
luxury lecherousness
according to the trick only as a joke, as is the custom

Enter BARNARDINE, PROVOST, CLAUDIO [*muffled*] *and* JULIET

DUKE Which is that Barnardine?
PROVOST   This, my lord.
DUKE There was a friar told me of this man.
       Sirrah, thou art said to have a stubborn soul
       That apprehends no further than this world,
       And squar'st thy life according. Thou'rt condemned: 475
       But, for those earthly faults, I quit them all,
       And pray thee take this mercy to provide
       For better times to come. Friar, advise him,
       I leave him to your hand. – What muffled fellow's that?
PROVOST This is another prisoner that I saved,   480
       Who should have died when Claudio lost his head,
       As like almost to Claudio as himself.
                  [*He unmuffles Claudio*]
DUKE [*To Isabella*] If he be like your brother, for his sake
       Is he pardoned, and for your lovely sake
       Give me your hand, and say you will be mine,   485
       He is my brother too. But fitter time for that.
       By this Lord Angelo perceives he's safe;
       Methinks I see a quick'ning in his eye.
       Well, Angelo, your evil quits you well.
       Look that you love your wife: her worth, worth yours.   490
       I find an apt remission in myself;
       And yet here's one in place I cannot pardon,
       [*To Lucio*] You, sirrah, that knew me for a fool, a coward,
       One all of luxury, an ass, a madman:
       Wherein have I so deserved of you   495
       That you extol me thus?
LUCIO 'Faith, my lord, I spoke it but according to the trick: if you
    will hang me for it, you may – but I had rather it would please
    you I might be whipped.
DUKE Whipped first, sir, and hanged after.   500
       Proclaim it, provost, round about the city:
       If any woman wronged by this lewd fellow,
       As I have heard him swear himself there's one
       Whom he begot with child, let her appear,
       And he shall marry her. The nuptial finished,   505
       Let him be whipped and hanged.

The Duke reduces Lucio's sentence to marrying the prostitute who has borne his child. After advice, thanks and forgiveness to all the others, the Duke again proposes marriage to Isabella.

1 I do?

Will Isabella accept the Duke's proposal of marriage? Study this photograph of the Royal Shakespeare Company's 1974 production, and decide how 'your' Isabella would respond.

2 An epilogue?

Several Shakespeare plays have an epilogue: one character comes forward to address the audience, summing up the 'moral' of what they've just seen. Choose a character to speak an epilogue to *Measure for Measure*. Write a dozen lines for him or her.

3 *Exeunt*: a final image

In some productions, the characters leave the stage in pairs, obviously in a happy ending. In others, the ending is far less happy or clear. If you were directing the play, how would you stage the final moments? Work out how each character leaves the stage, and the very last image that the audience will see of your production of *Measure for Measure*.

---

cuckold deceived husband
punk prostitute
pressing to death killed by having stones heaped on the chest
restore marry

more behind yet to come
gratulate rewarding
place office, position
yet behind still to be told
meet fitting

LUCIO I beseech your highness, do not marry me to a whore. Your
    highness said, even now, I made you a duke: good my
    lord, do not recompense me in making me a cuckold.
DUKE Upon mine honour, thou shalt marry her.   510
    Thy slanders I forgive, and therewithal
    Remit thy other forfeits: take him to prison,
    And see our pleasure herein executed.
LUCIO Marrying a punk, my lord, is pressing to death, whipping, and
    hanging!   515
DUKE Slandering a prince deserves it.
    She, Claudio, that you wronged, look you restore.
    Joy to you, Mariana! Love her, Angelo!
    I have confessed her, and I know her virtue.
    Thanks, good friend Escalus, for thy much goodness;   520
    There's more behind, that is more gratulate.
    Thanks, provost, for thy care and secrecy,
    We shall employ thee in a worthier place.
    Forgive him, Angelo, that brought you home
    The head of Ragozine for Claudio's;   525
    Th'offence pardons itself. Dear Isabel,
    I have a motion much imports your good,
    Whereto, if you'll a willing ear incline,
    What's mine is yours, and what is yours is mine.
    So bring us to our palace, where we'll show   530
    What's yet behind that's meet you all should know.
                                                    [*Exeunt*]

Looking back at Act 5
Activities for groups or individuals

---

1 The City Gate (in pairs)

The whole of Act 5 takes place in front of Vienna's city gate. Some critics have argued that the gates symbolise the themes of sex and justice. Design the set for the act, incorporating some of that symbolism in your design. Work out how the Duke and his followers enter your set at the beginning of the act.

2 Measure for measure?

One meaning of the title is 'let the punishment fit the crime'. But does each wrongdoer get his or her just deserts?

Consider in turn: Angelo, Claudio, Lucio, Barnardine, Pompey, Mistress Overdone. Talk together about what you think of the justice or mercy they finally receive. What would your sentences be on each?

Do other characters get what they deserve? Consider Isabella, Juliet, Mariana, Kate Keepdown, the Duke.

3 Point of view

Modern directors are often accused of 'concept theatre' in which one dominant idea or concept affects every aspect of their production. Usually the 'accusers' have their own firm (but different) concept of how Shakespeare should be performed!

Imagine that you are a director. You wish to put on *Measure for Measure* from one of the following points of view:

- Marxist (money underlies every human/social relationship)
- Psychoanalytic (childhood experience underlies all adult behaviour)
- Feminist (from a woman's perspective, questioning male assumptions)
- New Historicist (plays reveal the historical period of their writing)
- Poetic-Aesthetic (the beauty of the language is what matters)
- Liberal humanist (individual freedom and human progress are the goals)
- Brechtian (remind the audience they are watching a political play).

Work out how 'your' concept would present Act 5. Act it out.

4 Five years on

Write a short story in which one character recalls, five years after the play's end, what has happened to each of the others.

5 Unveilings – in 'fast forward'

Elizabethans and Jacobeans relished the complex unravellings and disclosures at the end of plays.

Identify all the 'unveilings' in Act 5. Find a way of presenting them in a 'fast forward' version. Make it speedy but clear!

6 Imaginative re-creations

Artists, writers and composers throughout history have been creatively and imaginatively inspired by the *Measure for Measure* story. There are echoes in Verdi's opera *Tosca*, in Herman Melville's novel *Billy Budd* (and Benjamin Britten's opera based on Melville's story), in Gilbert and Sullivan's *Trial by Jury*. Holman Hunt's painting of Isabella and Claudio hangs in London's Tate Gallery. Bob Dylan's song 'Seven Curses' has the same 'monstrous ransom' ('She knew the judge had never spoken/She saw her father's body broken'). Wagner's opera *Das Liebesverbot* ('The Ban on Love') had a surprise ending: Isabella declared that she had loved Lucio from the start, and left the stage arm in arm with him!

Draft the outline of your own play, opera, novel or painting based on *Measure for Measure*.

7 What about Pompey?

Imagine that Pompey has been released from prison and witnesses the events of Act 5. Write or tell the story he relates to Froth that night.

8 Who has learned what?

Consider each major character in turn. Talk together about what you think each has learned in the course of the play (if anything).

9 A hasty ending?

Does Shakespeare round it off all too quickly? Argue for and against.

A problem play?

Measure for Measure has provoked more disagreement among critics than any other Shakespeare play. For every view expressed since its first recorded performance in 1604, there is an exactly opposite judgement. It does not fit neatly into conventional genres – 'comedy', 'tragedy', 'history' – so it has been called a tragi-comedy or dark comedy. It is most often referred to as a 'problem play' because its bitter nature and sardonic questioning of values leave audiences and readers perplexed and uncertain. All the judgements that follow have been made by well-known critics or directors.

'realistic' *v.* 'artificial'
'a very great comedy' *v.* 'pure and simple tragedy'
'like the parables of Jesus' *v.* 'a bitterly satirical play'
'wonderful sympathy' *v.* 'horrible'; 'repulsive'; 'hateful'
'a masterpiece of ethical drama' *v.* 'a reactionary fantasy'

Consider each pair of judgements in turn. Talk together about how and why you agree or disagree with the different viewpoints.

What is *Measure for Measure* about?

The story of *Measure for Measure* can be briefly told: 'Vincentio, Duke of Vienna, appoints Angelo to rule the city in his absence. Angelo condemns Claudio to death for fornication, but promises Isabella that he will lift the death sentence if she has sex with him. The Duke, disguised as a friar, substitutes Mariana for Isabella in Angelo's bed, saves Claudio and unmasks but pardons the corrupt Deputy.'

Such a bare outline does no justice to the rich complexity of Shakespeare's storytelling. 'What the play is about' has provoked a wide range of interpretations:

'a Christian allegory'
'a psychological study of repressed desire'
'a dramatised debate between justice and mercy'
'sexual obsessiveness, mixed guilt, abhorrence'
'a play about absolutes: restraint, chastity, authority'
'concerned with the emotional foundations of political structures'.

Identify three moments in the play to justify each interpretation.

Characters

A good actor can make any Shakespeare character seem to be an utterly believable flesh-and-blood human being with a fully lived past, but that does not mean that a character has to be fully consistent or 'fully rounded'. Characters can be full of contradictions. The characters in *Measure for Measure* have been viewed in very different ways by well-known critics:

Vincentio, Duke of Vienna   'Essentially a wise and noble man . . . a hero and good ruler'; 'True virtue, like true love, rests in the Duke'; 'an ever increasing mysterious dignity'; 'he has a divine quality'; *'Shifty'; 'unreasonable, implausible, sensational and stagey'; 'cold and self-important'; 'a cruel, offensive eavesdropper'; 'an irresponsible and libertine ruler'.*

Isabella   'An angel of light'; 'virgin sanctity'; 'moral grandeur'; 'saintly grace'; 'fair and virtuous'; 'perfect woman'; 'the heavenly purity of her mind . . . not even stained with one unholy thought'; *'Smug, vixenish, intolerant, selfish'; 'rancid about her rigid chastity'; 'pitiless, inhuman, hard as an icicle'; 'heartless'; 'a hypocrite'; 'a vicious sex-hysteric'.*

Angelo   'Vicious and hypocritical'; 'pharisaical pride'; 'does not know himself'; 'swiftly becomes an utter scoundrel'; 'self-righteous and unsubtle'; 'a lying self-deceiving fraud'; *'Not a conscious hypocrite, rather a man whose chief faults are self-deception and pride in his own self-righteousness'; 'childlike naivety about passion'; 'not an intrinsically evil person'.*

Claudio   'Portrayed by Shakespeare with unfailing sympathy and affection'; *'wavering'; 'disgusting'; 'detestable'.*

Lucio   'The most acute intelligence in the play'; *'a loose-minded vulgar wit'.*

Organise a class debate on 'How any character is viewed depends more on the beliefs and attitudes of the reader or spectator than on the intentions of the author or the performance of a particular actor'.

Invent a 'typical gesture' for each character in the play.

The writer in his time

Shakespeare reflected in his plays the world he knew. He might set the action in Rome or Denmark, but the values, beliefs and interests of his own times show through. *Measure for Measure* (written in 1603–4?) is set in Vienna, but is rich in evidence of the political, economic, social and literary concerns of early seventeenth-century England.

King James VI of Scotland and I of England

King James succeeded Queen Elizabeth in 1603. Some of his characteristics are echoed in *Measure for Measure*:

a He attempted secretly to observe his subjects (2.4.24–30)
b He intervened in criminal justice trials (5.1.350–531)
c He made last-minute reprieves of execution (5.1.483–91)
d He was said to dislike crowds (1.1.67–72)
e He cultivated a serious, scholarly image (3.2.124–6; 1.1.67–72)
f He claimed that he ruled too laxly in his Scottish reign (1.3.20–4)
g He denounced slanderers of princes (3.2.158–61)
h In 1603 he published *Basilikon Doron* ('The King's Gift'), setting out the qualities of the ideal ruler ('above all, let the measure of your love to everyone be according to the measure of his virtue').

Talk together about whether you think Shakespeare was consciously flattering King James in the passages above.

The Bible

Throughout *Measure for Measure* are echoes of Jesus's Sermon on the Mount and other New Testament verses:

> 'Judge not, that ye be not judged. For with what judgement ye judge, ye shall be judged; and with what measure ye mete, it shall be measured to you again.' (Matthew 7: 1–2)

> 'Ye have heard that it hath been said, An eye for an eye, and a tooth for a tooth. . . . But I say unto you, Love your enemies, bless them that curse you, do good to them that hate you.' (Matthew 5:38–44)

Read Jesus's Sermon on the Mount in Matthew chapters 5–7. Identify any verses which might have influenced Shakespeare.
Find lines in the play that echo each biblical quotation above.

Jacobean society: England 1603–4

- Some Puritan extremists abhorred prostitution so much that they advocated the death penalty for offenders (it became law in 1650).
- A Proclamation in 1603 ordered the demolition of property in London's suburbs to prevent the spread of plague.
- With a new king only recently enthroned, there was a constant fear of social disaffection. The Gunpowder Plot occurred in 1605.
- The Lord Chamberlain, the Bishop of Winchester and some theatre-owners also owned property leased for brothels.
- In Essex, an adult stood a one in four chance of being accused of a sexual offence at some point during their lifetime.
- Most people probably believed that they might be eternally damned if they committed a mortal sin (like fornication).
- The City of London prepared a lavish ceremonial Royal Entry to London for King James. Elaborate triumphal arches were built.
- A couple intending to marry could simply agree to a 'contract' (or 'pre-contract'): a verbal agreement with or without witnesses. It served to establish the couple as man and wife.
- Sexual intercourse between contracted couples was common. Many never married in church. Only in 1752 did a church wedding become the only legally valid form of marriage.
- It was a time of roaring inflation. The economic remedy proposed was *per pro pari* ('measure for measure'): holding the intrinsic value of coins absolutely rigid. There was great fear of forgery.
- The king 'touched' sick people at Christmas and Easter to cure them of the 'King's Evil' (scrofula). He simultaneously handed out Angels: coins with an angel on one side and a trading ship on the other.

The following questions provoke great disagreement. What's your view? Support your argument with evidence from the script.

- Can you deduce facts about Shakespeare's England from the play?
- Does the play have elements relevant to all people in every age?
- Does the play reveal Shakespeare's own beliefs (for example, on morality)?
- Do you think the play criticises or supports aspects of Jacobean society (for example, the King, the law, the criminals, women's status, religion)?
- Do all writers inevitably reflect in their work the beliefs, issues and values of the times in which they live?

The powerful and the powerless

Charles Marowitz, writer and director, has experimented with rewriting Shakespeare plays. His version of *Measure for Measure* omits all the 'lower-class' characters, allows Isabella to be raped by Angelo, and has Claudio executed. Isabella's story is publicly disbelieved, and in the final scene the three rulers sit down to dinner together, joking about what has happened. All the language is Shakespeare's, but it has been re-ordered and reallocated. Here is that final scene:

(The following dialogue is permeated with a gaiety and crudity that belies all we know of these characters.)

DUKE   *(Mimicking the lower-classes)* What news abroad i' the world?

ANGELO   *(Mock guiltily, also with put-on voice)* Sir, I have been an unlawful bawd time out of mind, but yet I will be content to be a lawful hangman. I would be glad to receive some instruction from me fellow partner.

ESCALUS   *(Laughing at ANGELO's imitation; mock-astonished)* A bawd, sir? *(To DUKE).* Fie upon him, he will discredit our mystery.

ANGELO   'Faith, my lord, I spoke it but according to the trick. If you will hang me for it, you may. But I had rather it would please you I might be whipped.

(All fall about with laughter.)

DUKE   Whipped first, sir, and hanged after. *(This tops last joke and all explode with even greater laughter.)* Proclaim it, Provost, round about the city, If any woman wronged by this lewd fellow, As I have heard him swear himself there's one Whom he begot with child – let her appear, And he shall marry her.

ANGELO   *(Acting craven)* I beseech your highness, do not marry me to a whore. Marrying a punk, my Lord, is pressing to death, whipping *and* hanging.

DUKE   *(Pouring wine over ANGELO's head)* Slandering a prince deserves it.

(All laugh uproariously and carry on clowning, eating and drinking through.)

(Fade out)

In small groups read through the piece of dialogue, then talk about the changes that Marowitz has made.

- Do you find anything shocking about the dialogue?
- There is a lot of laughter in this scene – are the lines funny?
- How would you describe Escalus, Angelo and the Duke as they are portrayed here?
- What relationship do the rulers have with the ruled?
- What does this version reveal about the politics of the play?

Two aspects of government

There was much debate about the ethics and nature of 'good government' in Jacobean England. King James I had just published his own work on the subject, *Basilikon Doron* (1603), and Machiavelli's *The Prince* (Italy, 1513) was influential. The illustration opposite is based on a conventional depiction of the relationship between ruler and state, using the metaphor of the 'body politic'. The ruler is quite literally the 'head' of state. All is harmonious.

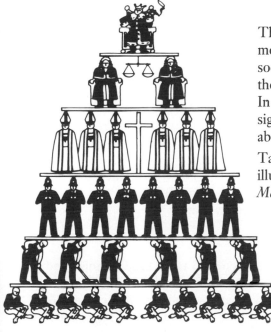

The second illustration shows a modern artist's 'reading' of the social structure contained within the play.

In what ways does it differ significantly from the image used above?

Talk together about the two illustrations and relate them to *Measure for Measure*.

Justice and mercy

1 Crime and punishment, law and order

References to different types of 'Justice' are frequently made in *Measure for Measure*. Corporal and capital punishment are central elements of the government's policy on law and order. In groups of about ten, share out the following lines and learn them. Devise a presentation through tableaux, mime or other movement, using the lines.

Liberty plucks justice by the nose
Thus can the demi-god, authority
Let him be whipped and hanged
whipped first, sir, and hanged after
Slander to th'state/Away with him to prison!
Away with him to prison/Lay bolts enough on him
we must not make a scarecrow of the law
Away with him to death!
An Angelo for Claudio, death for death
Take him to prison, officer/Correction and instruction must both work
of two usuries, the merriest was put down, and the worser allowed by order of law
the law hath not been dead, though it hath slept
within these three days his head to be chopped off!
My absolute power and place here in Vienna
To th'rack with him! We'll touze you/Joint by joint, but will know his purpose
I have seen corruption boil and bubble/Till it o'errun the stew
Show your sheep-biting face, and be hanged an hour!
Immediate sentence then, and sequent death

2 A trial

In the end, Angelo is excused his attempted rape, false promise and attempted murder. Claudio, too, is let off. Yet Lucio is sent to prison, and as far as we know Pompey and other assorted 'low-life' characters remain in prison. Who would *you* want to put on trial and imprison at the end of the play? Choose from the list of characters below, and prepare a prosecution case against them:

- Angelo
- Pompey
- the Duke
- Mistress Overdone
- Escalus
- Lucio.

Give each the opportunity to defend themselves.

3 Measure for measure? (in small groups)

The traditional 'reading' (interpretation) of *Measure for Measure* sets out to demonstrate that an absolute Justice is eventually fused with Mercy in the course of the play. It provides an object lesson in 'good government'. Such a reading can be represented in this way:

| false justice | → | merciless rigour | → | merciful grace |

- What evidence can you find that 'Justice' is tempered with 'Mercy'?
- Do you think there is 'resolution' at the end of the play, to show that Mercy does indeed temper Justice?
- Are any laws repealed?
- Are Angelo, Escalus and the Duke shown to have changed their authoritarian approach to government by the end of the play?

Find ways of presenting your thoughts on Justice and Mercy in the play using only quotations taken from the script. Can you balance measure for measure?

To th'rack with him!

Sex and sexuality

1 Aspects of sexuality

At the heart of *Measure for Measure* are controversial questions about sexuality, 'immorality' and marriage. In the nineteenth century, polite society found it all so unpleasant that *Measure for Measure* was rarely performed. But the play's ambiguity about sex, its contradictions and openness to interpretation, have found increasing favour in the second half of the twentieth century.

Copy the following diagram on to a large sheet of paper and define what aspects of sexuality each character represents.

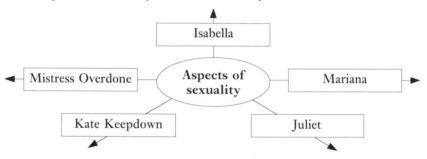

The following quotations are all said by men about female characters. Match each to one of the characters named on your diagram.

> marrying a punk . . . is pressing to death, whipping and hanging!
> her plenteous womb/Expresseth his full tilth and husbandry
> ever your fresh whore and your powdered bawd.
> neither maid, widow, nor wife
> when maidens sue/Men give like the gods
> she is fast my wife
> a wench with child . . . the rotten medlar
> a very virtuous maid/And to be shortly of a sisterhood
> Madam Mitigation

Present the lines to the rest of the class,
either   diagrammatically on large sheets of paper,
   or   dramatically, using tableaux or choral speaking.

2 Different readings

Attitudes to sex in *Measure for Measure* can be read in entirely opposite ways.

a The traditional reading: widespread immorality in Vienna, particularly in the lower classes, will lead to lawlessness in the state as a whole, corrupting the better-off classes. The government needs to step in and sort it out.

b A recent challenge to that reading: the rulers of Vienna are corrupt, and abuse their power. In order to deflect attention away from themselves, they say that lechery is a problem and inflict oppressive laws on the people. They make sexuality central to their struggle for political control; women in particular are exploited.

Copy the table below on to a large sheet of paper. Complete the right- and left-hand columns with details of possible opposing readings of each woman's sexuality.

Reading 1 (deviant behaviour needs changing by law)		Reading 2 (corruption comes from the rulers; women are exploited by men in power)
Isabella's denial of her sexuality is unnatural. The Duke leads her back to normal sexual relations.	ISABELLA	
	MISTRESS OVERDONE	*She's struggling to survive under harsh laws and poverty... ...male attitudes...*
	JULIET	
	MARIANA	*...dutiful subjection to male authority... ...dependence..*
	KATE KEEPDOWN	

The language of *Measure for Measure*

1 Measure for measure

On every page of the play, the title is exemplified in the language. A character weighs or compares one thing or person against another ('An Angelo for Claudio, death for death'; 'We cannot weigh our brother with ourself'). The process begins in the opening scene when the Duke says that Escalus's knowledge outweighs his own (1.1.5–7). Many, but not all of these comparisons are antitheses: balanced contrasts achieved by setting words and ideas in opposition to each other ('To sue to live, I find I seek to die / And seeking death find life' 3.1.42–3).

Take any ten pages of the script at random. Identify at least one example of this 'weighing process' on each page. Find a way to represent your findings – through a short play or a story, or as a series of illustrations.

2 Personification

When the Duke complains: 'Liberty plucks Justice by the nose', he is using personification: turning abstractions into human beings. Make an illustration of the Duke's words, then find further examples of personification in the script and portray them in other ways.

3 Keywords?

Certain words re-echo through the play: *seeming, mercy, justice, liberty, restraint, authority, blood, grace, sense, scope.* Identify how often each word is used, and who uses it. Display your findings. Are there other 'key' words?

4 Imagery

Measure for Measure contains striking imagery: words or phrases which evoke emotionally laden pictures. Notable examples are forgery (pages 5, 63 and 67), pregnancy (pages 25, 61, 133), corruption and disease (pages 11, 123, 159). But some critics argue that the play appeals more to the intellect than to the imagination or emotions. Talk together about the view that 'ideas, not images, predominate in the play'.

5 Echoes of the Bible

Measure for Measure is rich in biblical allusions, particularly from Jesus's Sermon on the Mount (see page 176).

Make a two-column list, setting all the biblical allusions you can find against the corresponding passages in Shakespeare's script. Write a sermon or political speech on a topic of current concern incorporating as many of the quotations as you can.

6 Puns and malapropisms

A pun is made when the same sound or word has different meanings. When Isabella says to Angelo, 'I am come to know your pleasure', she means 'pleasure' as 'intention'; he interprets it as 'sexual desire'.

Malapropisms are language muddles (see page 34). Elbow uses 'malefactors' for 'benefactors'.

Find one or two further examples of puns or malapropisms. Devise a dramatic presentation to display their ambiguity.

7 Irony

The whole play is deeply ironic in its concern with false appearances, disguise, deceit and the unmasking of hypocrisy. Characters are unaware of the true or deeper meanings of language or events (for example, Angelo does not grasp the real significance of the Duke's words 'be you judge of your own cause'). Talk together about what you understand by irony, using examples from the script (for example, page 140).

8 Two types of language?

The language of the play changes dramatically at 3.1.152. Up to that point the language is sensuously powerful and active. That vivid, fervent language then becomes much more passive and prosaic. Wordy exposition in prose replaces eloquent and energetic blank verse. There are far fewer memorably poetic and expressive passages.

Read 3.1.135–75. Talk together about how you detect the kind of linguistic change outlined above. Explore possible reasons for it: for example, do the intricacies of the Duke's plotting require the shift to expository prose? Is it because the characters change from realistic human beings to mere ciphers used to work out the plot?

Setting and staging

The two photographs show the stage set for the Royal Shakespeare Company's 1987 production of *Measure for Measure*. The two sets are quite literally the reverse of each other; set A rotates to reveal set B for the appropriate scenes:

A

For which scenes do you think set A would be used, and for which set B?

What 'interpretation' of the play do these two sets encourage?

B